# How to Partner Dance Socially

# How to Partner Dance Socially

*For students and teachers*

*For complete beginners and experienced dancers*

Dr Duncan James

# Table of Contents

Simply Start Partner Dancing Now!..................................................................................................1
How to Use This Book.......................................................................................................................2
Being a Dance Student......................................................................................................................3
Being a Dance Teacher.....................................................................................................................6
Lead-Follow is the Core of Partner Dancing....................................................................................12
Partner Dance Lead-Follow Practice...............................................................................................16
A Course of Lessons in Ballroom Dancing......................................................................................19
Learning Foxtrot (Ballroom).............................................................................................................20
    Foxtrot Complete Beginners (Slow Basic) (Ballroom).................................................................21
    Foxtrot Complete Beginners (Slow Slow Quick Quick) (Ballroom)..............................................27
    Foxtrot Beginners Leader Solo Practice (Ballroom)....................................................................34
Learning Quickstep (Ballroom).........................................................................................................35
    Quickstep Complete Beginners (Slow Basic) (Ballroom)............................................................36
    Quickstep Complete Beginners (Slow Slow Quick Quick) (Ballroom).........................................38
    Quickstep Beginners Leader Solo Practice (Ballroom)...............................................................41
    All Slows in Quickstep (Ballroom)................................................................................................43
        Quickstep Improvers All Slows Introduction (All Slows in Quickstep) (Ballroom)....................44
        Quickstep Improvers Slow Stepping Offset and Promenade (All Slows in Quickstep) (Ballroom)
...............................................................................................................................................45
        Quickstep Improvers Pivot Turn Back on Left (All Slows in Quickstep) (Ballroom)..................48
        Quickstep Improvers Pivot Turn Back on Right (All Slows in Quickstep) (Ballroom)................50
        Quickstep Improvers Pivot Turn Back on Both (All Slows in Quickstep) (Ballroom).................52
        Quickstep Improvers Follower Zig Zag (All Slows in Quickstep) (Ballroom).............................54
        Quickstep Improvers Leader and Follower Zig Zag (All Slows in Quickstep) (Ballroom)..........57
Learning Waltz (Ballroom)................................................................................................................58
    Waltz Complete Beginners (Ballroom).........................................................................................59
    Waltz Beginners Dancing Closer (Ballroom)...............................................................................65
    Waltz Beginners Solo Practice (Ballroom)...................................................................................68
    Waltz Beginners Solo Practice (Extra Exercises for Leader) (Ballroom).....................................70
    Waltz Improvers 360 Turn to the Right (Ballroom)......................................................................71
    Waltz Improvers 360 Turn to the Left (Ballroom)........................................................................75
    Waltz Improvers 360 Turn Both Ways (Ballroom).......................................................................77
    Waltz Improvers All Forwards (Ballroom)....................................................................................79
    Waltz Improvers Curved Basic (Ballroom)...................................................................................81
    Waltz Improvers Leader Backwards (Ballroom)..........................................................................87
    Waltz Improvers Leader Curve Backwards (Ballroom)...............................................................89
    Waltz Advanced Using Rumba as Variation (Ballroom)..............................................................91
A Course of Lessons in Latin Dancing.............................................................................................93
Learning Rumba (Latin)...................................................................................................................94
    Rumba Complete Beginners (Latin).............................................................................................95
    Rumba Beginners Forward-and-Back Basic (Latin)....................................................................99
    Rumba Beginners Slow Turns and Dance Arounds (Latin)......................................................102
    Rumba Beginners Rotating Forward-and-Back Basic (Latin)...................................................105
    Rumba Improvers Travelling Side Basic (Latin)........................................................................107
Learning Salsa (Latin)....................................................................................................................109
    Salsa Complete Beginners (Latin).............................................................................................110
    Salsa Beginners Forward-and-Back Basic (Latin)....................................................................113

- Learning Cha Cha (Latin) .................................................................................................... 115
  - Cha Cha Complete Beginners (Latin) .............................................................................. 116
  - Cha Cha Beginners Forward-and-Back Basic (Latin) ...................................................... 119
  - Cha Cha Beginners Side Basic (Latin) ............................................................................. 121
  - Cha Cha Beginners New Yorkers (Latin) ......................................................................... 123
  - Cha Cha Beginners Criss Cross Basic (Latin) .................................................................. 126
- Latin Solo Practice ................................................................................................................ 129
  - Latin Beginners Follower Solo Practice ........................................................................... 130
  - Latin Beginners Leader Solo Practice .............................................................................. 133
  - Latin Improvers Follower Solo Practice ........................................................................... 135
  - Latin Improvers Leader Solo Practice .............................................................................. 137
- Latin Improvers Cross Body Move ....................................................................................... 139
- Latin Improvers One or Two ................................................................................................. 143
- Copyright and Video Download Link .................................................................................... 144

# *Simply Start Partner Dancing Now!*

This quick-start page is aimed at complete beginners.

The simplest ballroom dance I teach is foxtrot (go to page 21).
*Estimated learning time: 30 minutes.*

`https://youtu.be/FL7xj8-OEUw`

The next-simplest ballroom dance I teach is waltz (go to page 59).
*Estimated learning time: 60 minutes.*

`https://youtu.be/vVGeyhYoULM`

The simplest latin dance I teach is rumba (go to page 95).
*Estimated learning time: 45 minutes.*

`https://youtu.be/QxCCL9tbslQ`

Questions? Want more?

Continue reading this book to learn more.
*Including links to many more lessons on YouTube.*

You are welcome to email me at drduncanjames@gmail.com for learning advice.

Keep it smooth;
Keep it relaxed;
Don't force your partner;
Feel the rhythm;
Keep it safe.

# *How to Use This Book*

Any questions or comments or just want to chat? Email me (the author) at drduncanjames@gmail.com and I'll do my best to reply.

This book teaches a social form of partner dancing typical to England. Many (perhaps a majority) of people dance the way that is taught in this book. Note that it is more subtle and less structured (although no less musical and no less romantic) than the styles that might be seen in dancing competitions. I have danced my way all around the world with this style and I have found that it is familiar to and works with most dancers: Perhaps because it is a musical, intuitive and informal approach. Some formal dancers find my approach refreshing and particularly musical; Others dislike the freedom and prefer to dance set moves.

This book has no photographs nor diagrams. However, most chapters have a dedicated video with recordings from many angles; In addition most of the key teaching points are demonstrated or described in voiceover. These videos are linked from the text and there is no extra charge. Some people choose to simply use the videos on their own and not purchase this book.

This is both a self-learning partner dancing book and a manual for teachers.

I have taught dance on average twice a week for over two decades (from approximately 1995 to 2015). From my third class I was making notes on what was most effective and what questions and problems students had. I have gained inspiration from other teachers and also used my training as a scientist to develop and test unique teaching techniques of my own. My notes, and two years testing with volunteers to ensure everything also works for independent learning, have enabled me to write this "Partner Dance Handbook".

It is designed to get you dancing as quickly as possible, in a safe way around a crowded dance floor. The focus is on "fun and social dancing" and not "competition and show dancing".

Some unique approaches are covered that mean you can create a wide variety of moves and variations to help you interpret the music with surprisingly little learning.

If you are a complete beginner you might start with the "complete beginners lessons" in foxtrot, waltz and rumba. These are particularly designed to act as introductions to partner dance even if you have never danced before. You should be able to choose one and be dancing in a fun way with an authentic style in time with the music within an hour. Safety aspects if dancing on a crowded floor are also covered so you could join in a social dance if you wish.

If you are a more advanced dancer you might browse and find good starting points. Because the teaching approach is unique I suggest you still do some of the complete beginners lessons to get some new perspectives. Students report that my lessons particularly help them develop better connection with their partner, improvise outside of the standard moves and interpret and improvise to the music better.

If you are a teacher then reading the chapter about teaching and then skim reading the chapters on either waltz or rumba (including the latin cross body move chapter) should give you an overview of how I teach partner dance.

There are a matching set of free video lessons on my YouTube channel https://www.youtube.com/drduncanjames so you can see things which are difficult to explain in words or pictures. The videos are branded as "ticket2dance" so if you discovered this book via a video or from one of his dance lessons (which are also often called "ticket2dance") you are in the right place.

Direct links to each video are given where appropriate in the text. You can also find the videos by browsing for them on my YouTube channel.

Alternatively you can download the videos using the link on the copyright page. However, YouTube in general offers a smooth viewing experience with good playback controls if you have access to it.

You can "follow" me on Amazon to get updates about my new books. If you enjoy this book, a rating or review will help other readers discover it; thank you. If this book is not working for you then you are welcome to email me at drduncanjames@gmail.com and I will try to fix the problem for you and, by extension, for future readers.

# *Being a Dance Student*

All this is general advice and depending on your learning style you might find alternatives that work better for you.

## Video Lesson Tips for the Free Videos on YouTube

You can use the rewind button to keep trying things again: I specifically designed the videos with this in mind because I think it is easier to rewind over things you have already seen than for too much repetition to mean you have to go forwards and then possibly skip something important.

The numbers in the videos correspond to the numbers in the book lesson plans.

Each numbered section of a video usually has a number of repeats with different things emphasised. So, be careful of using a replay button during a scene as maybe a repeat might be about to happen anyway and it might cover a different aspect that will help you more.

You do not need to do exactly the same size steps or exactly the same positions you see in the videos. If your foot is in a slightly different place or at a slightly different angle it is fine.

While learning from videos I suggest that you learn one dance at a time. Spend some time learning the complete beginners video for one dance before moving onto another type of dance.

When I demonstrate on the video you might join in or copy at the same time. You might just watch. You might try doing the basic step while I do the more advanced move so you can more easily see the differences. The only right way is the way that works for you at that time.

If you do copy straight away I recommend stopping and starting again if it feels wrong to avoid practising a mistake and making the mistake feel natural.

Does something feel odd? I strongly recommend you immediately stop. Then take a breath and start again. For people I have taught, continuing to dance when something feels odd has often led to bad habits. It can be frustrating to keep stopping but I think this is less frustrating then developing a bad habit that is then difficult to break.

If you are copying something on the video and it goes wrong you might stop and join back in. Or you might just keep going and try to get back in time. Find what works for you. Some people like to watch it for a while and really get a feeling for what is happening and then try joining in.

If you are doing free practice (not just copying someone on the video) and it goes wrong then you can just stop and start again. You might have to do this a lot of times. You might have to stop after just a few seconds. And then keep starting again 10, 20, 50 or 100 times. In general, my experience of teaching dance is that fighting to make it work is not a good strategy. I often see students patiently restart for up to half an hour and then suddenly it all works. The students in the room who kept going even though it was going wrong are often really struggling at this point as they have been developing muscle memory of the wrong thing. The students willing to keep restarting end up typically doing best in the long run.

In the videos we often demonstrate at a slight angle so you can see the leader and the follower. This can make the right and left foot look slightly different even if they are doing the same thing. We often also do demonstrations that are not at an angle to help overcome this problem. If we demonstrated without a slight angle it would be more difficult to see both of us on the screen.

The timing is often learnt in combination with the steps. A breakthrough can be when you really start to sense that the underlying rhythm is the same all the time.

Do you want more practice during one of the lessons? Simple! Pause the video and put on a song to practice to! You might use one of the ticket2dance demo dance videos so you can see another couple dancing at the same time to remind you of the timing and other things as you practice.

## The Leader Can Stand Still in Latin

The leader can always stand still and let the follower carry on. This is an actual fashionable thing to do and just needs the leader to have the confidence to stand there posing. Perhaps the follower could slowly dance around the leader. Perhaps the follower could then stop and then you both start dancing again (using your "stop and start again" skills).

I have used this for couples learning together where the leader is struggling and the follower wants to be stretched. I often need to remind the leader that no one is watching them and even if someone does glance their way they are going to be watching the follower dance around and not the leader standing still. It looks like a legitimate move (which in fact I consider it to be as I use it quite a bit).

## Does the Leader Have to Start With the Left?

No. And in fact I think it is better to use weight changes to find yourself on the same foot and start however you want, feeling what seems appropriate for each song.

## There are an Infinite Number of Possible Moves

I recommend that you eventually start to see the moves taught in lessons as guidelines and useful structures for initial learning. Dance in time with your partner and stay together. Let the leader come up with the moves and the follower can just follow wherever the dancing goes. Perhaps the follower will contribute some leading as well. Moves are a way to learn. Moves are not necessarily the final aim and definitely they are not the way I dance myself: Instead I improvise.

## Beginners Can Lead With Their Voice

Beginner leaders could simply say what they are about to do to help the follower. I will still do this sometimes when social dancing as it is easy and effective. So, if you are really struggling to lead something maybe just start saying it out loud to your partner a little bit before (work out between you a good time to say it) so that you can get on with enjoying the dancing!

## Small Spaces

If practising in a small space consider taking small steps to give space for more repeats of the steps before you run out of room. Once you go social dancing perhaps try stretching out to go faster. If you find that difficult initially, remember the outside lane (nearest the edge) at a social dance is for beginners and so if it takes you a few songs to start taking larger steps that is fine and advanced dancers can simply overtake you on the towards the centre of the dance floor.

## Hips in Latin

There are lots of fancy ways of moving your hip in latin dancing. For the long term sake of my hips I dance latin fairly simply. You might choose to do more hip movement in your own dancing. The simple way I dance is also a benefit as it is easier for students to copy when I am teaching and easier for beginners to dance themselves.

## Rise-and-Fall

I do not really discuss rise-and-fall as this is supposed to be simpler social dancing. It does get some mention in discussion of quicks and sometimes I demonstrate using rise-and-fall even if I don't talk about it.

## Side-Steps

A side-step is not taught during the second step of waltz as I feel it discourages lead-follow and creates one more thing to remember. This is another pragmatic decision to make a basic form of waltz that is quick and easy to learn and does not teach bad habits.

## A Piece of Paper in Latin

In the latin dances the use of a piece of paper is to make it easier to copy what is happening. I have found this to be very effective. I do mention in some places that the steps can be stretched and that the piece of paper is only a general guideline: this is generally true and I intend the piece of paper to be an "exaggeration" or "simplification" of dancing which is actually less rigid.

## Turning into the First Step of a Turn in Ballroom

In the ballroom dances I am teaching a slight turn on the first step forwards going into a turn whereas many teachers encourage this to happen on a straight line so the turn is more emphasised on the second step. In my experience a slight turn on the first step is necessary for many people with mobility issues (which I find is probably most people). Professional dancers are able to use core strength and well exercised leg muscles and tendons to turn tightly on the second step but I do not believe it is a good choice for most beginners. More advanced dancers often still do a curve on the first step but with a movement of the upper body (often called cbm). Ultimately, I see the slight turn a lot in social dancing so it seems a legitimate choice to teach beginners.

## Contra-Body-Movement

You might be aware of contra-body-movement. I have seen this with different names in many different styles of dancing. I chose to introduce it in different places at different times in different dances and not follow a standard approach. If I have a student willing to learn very slowly then I introduce it very early similar to the way some forms of Argentine tango do in order to compensate for the turning action of the forward step.

## "But Something is Different to How I Learnt it Elsewhere"

This is what many students say to me. My answer is that this is normal. Different teachers teach differently. Personally I encourage you to take everything anyone tells you (including what I say) as merely a suggestion. Find what works for you. Try different ideas out. Test them. See what feels comfortable for you. See what feels comfortable for your partner. Decide what styles you like. Develop your personal style. Make up your own ideas. Have fun!

# Being a Dance Teacher

### "Join in or Watch or do Something Else"

When I teach I encourage my students to make personal choices during the lesson. I allow them to choose whether to join in with a demonstration. Or whether to just watch. Or I am fine with a student doing something else. Sometimes students like to dance the basic step while I demonstrate something else so they can more easily see the difference. Alternatively, some students might want to skip repetition of a particular move and instead repeat something they found difficult earlier in the lesson. My only request is that if doing something different they consider moving to the side or back so it is not so visually off-putting for other students.

### Student Partner Feedback

At the start of a class you can ask followers to give feedback to the leaders and obviously encourage leaders to do the same for followers. I may nominate a particular day to be "follower feedback day" or "leader feedback day" to help with group learning but I may not do this if I feel the class are in very different situations in their personal learning. I will often model an interaction between a leader and a follower to show how these discussions can be positive experiences. Example ways that followers might describe the lead include:- too early, too late, timing good, too weak, too strong, strength good, not clear because hands moving even when there is not a lead, etc.

### The "Wrong" Problem

I try to never say something is wrong. I believe that dancing is a fun activity where it does not matter what we look like but just that we are enjoying ourselves without disturbing others. So, suppose someone is learning waltz and a particular movement that someone is doing is not harming anyone else but is not typical to waltz: then I will generally say something like "great dancing, I like the way you are trying different ways of moving but to make it more like waltz you could..." And in general conversation during the class I will try to say: "Is this waltz?" This is instead of: "Is this correct?". The emphasis in my teaching is to see all dancing as good and give feedback in the form of "safety advice" or "suggestions for more authentic styling for a particular style of dancing".

### A Class of Individuals

I have found that an impossible balancing act in a group class is addressing everyone's individual needs and also giving the group as a whole a good shared experience. Sometimes I have taught a class and worked really hard at giving everyone individual feedback and when I do this I find the lesson can become so fragmented it is barely a group class any more. And if I just focus on group goals I find individual issues might not get addressed enough. I try to find a "least worst" balance between these two teaching approaches for every class.

### How Many Partners to Move on Each Time?

If a class is working constructively together I will generally just move everyone on one at a time. If a class has some issues such as some learning-style clashes I will try to keep saying a different number: this makes it less obvious when I pick a particular number to keep certain people apart. I have seen some teachers always move on people 2 every time: be aware that if you have an even number of couples in the class this means any given student will only have danced with half the possible number of partners they could have during the entire lesson: so in this case I recommend sometimes calling an odd number such as 1 or 3 to give everyone a chance to dance with everyone.

## 3 to 5 Minutes

During the regular practice time in the class I try to play music for at least 3 to 5 minutes without me interrupting. I have found this is (on average) a popular time to give students time to work on the learning on their own. If the gaps are shorter than this I get complaints that I am interfering too much. If the gaps are longer I find people want more input.

## Learning Intention

I try to share a clear "learning intention" at the start of every class. This means explaining what improvements or learning I am planning for during the lesson. The reason I find this important is that some people have a learning style where they seem to benefit from knowing where the class is going. Definitely some people don't care and consider it wasted time. So, I try to be brief and maybe just spend 20 seconds explaining.

## Exaggerated Demonstrations

As a dance teacher I often exaggerate my stepping to make it clearer for my students to see. This generally means my styling is not typical for the dance. For this reason I try to remind my students every 15 minutes or so that this is an issue and demonstrate briefly without the exaggeration.

## Move Around

A great lesson I learnt once was to stand in different positions during the lesson. The reason I do this is partly to keep things more dynamic and help the students maintain good concentration. I also think it is a way of dealing with things like line-of-sight when students watch me demonstrating, for example it prevents one student having a pillar in the way for the entire class and not saying anything.

## Point With Your Whole Hand

If I point at something I like to have my hand open with my fingers loose. I then do a kind-of wave with my fingers with the arm directed towards where I want to point. I find students like this "softer" approach and it prevents the many negative emotions that are associated with a single-finger point entering my class.

## Just an Example

If I teach a sequence I make sure that I mention that the sequence is just an example. This is because some students have a preconception, perhaps from other learning, that the order a teacher demonstrates a skill in is the one it has to be done in. I encourage my students to be flexible and either experiment with different orders of doing moves/movements or simply let go and improvise in an unplanned way while dancing outside the class.

## My Problem not the Student's

If a student is finding something difficult I will usually first demonstrate and/or explain it at least one more time and give them space to ask questions or practice if they want to. Then, if the student is still finding it difficult I usually try to think of a simpler exercise that just practises one element of the problem move/skill. I will then typically keep breaking it down and finding a smaller thing to practice until they have success (and I try to use my intuition to guess the small skill that is the thing they are finding difficult). This is a universal approach I now use as a challenge to myself to take responsibility for the teaching (and not expect too much of the student).

## Resisting the Temptation to Help

Once people have begun a particular practice exercise (one that I am not leading) I try to spend spend up to 2 or 3 minutes just observing. If someone interrupts with a question I might say: "Not now, I'm watching carefully." Then I might go around and give individual feedback using descriptive praise to reinforce things like thoughtfulness, taking time, thinking, not rushing, authentic styling and so on. Then I might drift into a teaching role. Obviously I might break from this approach in some cases, for example if someone is repeatedly doing it wrong and not realising but even then I try to be patient.

I would say one of the two main exceptions to this is with a complete beginners lesson where we are pushing on fast with the learning, students expect to get lots of input at the start and I am trying to get the students dancing to a whole song as quickly as possible. In a complete beginners lesson I am going to just jump in after about 20 seconds and start giving lots of quick-fire advice.

The second main exception is with an established class. I will know my students and then I will often go and give individual help immediately to someone to make best use of the time.

## Allowing Mistakes

Related to the principle of allowing time at the start without interfering I also try to not fix mistakes with too many "learning tricks". I have found the same as has also been found by researchers: too many tricks to fix problems during learning can cause a student to struggle when they try to use the skill in "real life". Therefore I will often avoid the "quick fix" and simply give practical help and then let the student keep practising and trying to overcome the problem. (This means that many of the things I learnt in my early years as a teacher I no longer use!)

## Descriptive Praise

Descriptive praise is a way to add value to praise and help the student be empowered to develop further on their own. I try to eliminate words such as good, fine, excellent, great and so on. Instead I try to use specifics and don't slip in a "brilliant" at the end to water down the specific. If this is difficult I might start a sentence with "I really like the way..." and then finish by pointing out something good.

## Differences

People use differences in movement to learn. So I like to highlight differences between movements to aid learning.

## Demonstration is an Important First Stage in my Teaching

I have had a lot of feedback from students that wanted to see the whole thing before then having it broken down as a teaching process. In some cases I find people are then too impatient and this damages their learning: however overall my experience is that the benefits of an early demonstration outweigh the downsides.

## A Skilled Demonstration Speeds up Learning

However, an unskilled demonstration is almost as good if the teacher provides a commentary on good/bad points and ways to improve it. This has been shown during research. I mainly use this with more advanced students. I find beginners can get confused as they may be concentrating on the look and not listening so much to the words (which I think is a legitimate choice if someone is new and probably quite overwhelmed) and so they might mistakenly think I'm demonstrating correctly.

## Forgetting is not the Same as not Trying

I feel strongly that teachers should not tell students off for forgetting to do something they learnt earlier. (1) I have often seen students who are clearly trying hard forget something in which case telling them off seems pointless negativity when there was no malice. (2) If I let the mistake go and wait I often find it was only temporary while they were focussing on the new thing. To clarify: I find that when learning a new thing some older skills might slip for a while due to the concentration on the new skill.

## Descriptive Feedback

I try to help students by observing characteristics of their movement and describing it to them. They may not be equipped to do it themselves. eg "I observe steps 2 and 3 are in time and step one is early, you have good relaxed legs and I see large movements in the shoulder that you might decrease at some point but I think look fine". I have often found that students then quickly fix things because they just didn't realise.

## Feedback Directs Attention

You are directing the learner's thoughts (and worries and emotional responses and thinking delays and so on) when you mention something. Be sure you want the student to be thinking about what you are about to say! Be mindful of where you are directing their attention!

## Real Life Conditions

Consider the likely range of conditions a skill will be used under... and make the lessons prepare for this full range. This is an important principle in my teaching and why with dancing I aim to get my students dancing around a crowded dance floor within minutes of starting to learn. If a class is small I often use chairs to make the dance floor really small for the start of the lesson to force them to learn not to collide and keep their dancing small. Once they have got that I'll give them more space for having more fun later in the lesson, but then their first experience (which for many students is the most memorable learning that "imprints" what their future dancing will look like) will have been in a situation where they have to watch for collisions.

## Contextual Learning (Versus Blocked Learning)

This is a principle that has been developed during research into learning. (1) Blocked learning means learning one thing at a time in big chunks (eg learning one move all lesson). (2) Contextual learning means learning many things at once in small chunks (eg covering two or three things in one lesson). Blocked learning has been shown to give great performance during the lesson, but poor retention and adaptability. Contextual learning has been shown to give OK performance during the lesson, but great retention and adaptability. I think this can be misunderstood in dance teaching because teachers do not realise that one move might involve multiple different skills. So, even if I only "teach one move" I will split it up into component skills and teach those separately and not as a single thing.

## Contextual Learning Additional Benefits

Contextual learning is thought to be good because (1) learners can compare and contrast different things. (2) Learners get extra practice at "starting cold" because they keep doing new things.

## Posture in 3

A simplified set of posture instructions that I often use are: (1) Stand up. (2) Lean your whole body (so don't just push your head forwards) so the weight is in balls of feet. (3) Bend your knees slightly.

## Leading Tips

Some tips on leading I like are: (1) A good follower has arms like bungee cords; (2) Lead follow can be practised by trying to be too soft, too hard and then just right; (3) Beginner leaders lead 99% of the dance, advanced leaders lead 51% of the dance; (4) You might open the palm of the follower's hand towards the direction of turn to make it more comfortable.

## The End of a Class

I like to close a lesson with interaction (with the class) perhaps by asking: "What would you like to do next lesson?" particularly because it helps me tune my teaching to the specific needs of a group.

## Questions

Here are some good questions to ask your students at the end of a class. (You could get people to do "secret voting" but all facing forward and doing a thumbs-up or thumbs-down in front of their chests.) I try to ask a few of these approximately once every four weeks so I can keep trying to improve my teaching: (1) Did it feel too easy? I think you need to be careful with this. People often do not realise the number of basic errors that are holding them back in their dancing. I will often talk about this issue after having the vote. Obviously I will try to talk about it in a positive way; perhaps emphasising some simple things we can still work on and how they will make their dancing more fun and varied. (2) Did it feel too difficult? If the answer to this is yes then I would almost always agree to slow down and repeat material. (3) Was there too much partner swapping? My personal experience is that it is good to change partners every 5 minutes at the start of a lesson, then leave people with the same partner for about 15 minutes later on, then return to changing every 5 minutes and then maybe do some very rapid partner swapping every minute towards the end. When leaving everyone with the same partner I try to watch how they are partnered up to be sure there are not "problem couples" stuck with each other. (4) Was there too little partner swapping? I often like to ask the same question in reverse another time just to get a better feeling for what people are thinking.

## Learning is Incremental

When you learn something you learn in stages. When I fully integrated this idea with my teaching I think it was the moment I suddenly became a much better teacher. If a student cannot do something then consider trying to work out the skill they need to learn first: Perhaps they need the ability to do large movements with their whole arm before then; isolating the hand and then; making the hand move to a particular position and then; repeatedly put the hand in position and remove it and only then; try to move the hand to that position on a particular beat of the bar. The lesson chapters cover this a lot already, even if they do not spell out that it is an "incremental" approach.

## Waiting for an Answer

If I ask a question I wait for an absolute minimum of 12 seconds (counting slowly in my head) before saying anything else. This is because although the answer might be obvious to me, it could be very complicated for the class. Anyway, my general approach in dance teaching is not to ask too many questions as I think it is not helpful: If I do ask a question and no one answers I typically answer it myself and move on so the class can get dancing again.

## Teaching a Mixed Ability Class

In my early days as a dance teacher I took feedback from students personally if they said it was "too difficult" or "too easy". My simple piece of advice now is to realise you cannot make a class right for everyone. (1) Unless you have multiple different levels of class through the evening (which I am not typically a fan of because it can break up the social experience and rarely feels appropriate to me for the smaller "village hall" type settings where classes are often taught) it will obviously be too difficult for some and too easy for others. (2) Remember that many people who think the class is too easy are overestimating their own ability and still don't understand the basics. It rarely goes down well if I tell them this so I try to be tactful. I then find that they either continue coming (and complain to me every few weeks) or simply stop coming (perhaps just paying to join in the social dancing after the classes). (3) If I have a solid core of regular students that have been coming for while I usually give them priority in deciding what we do in class. However, I might at some point talk to them as a group and ask them if we can go back to simpler things to allow new people to join. (4) I often use special "complete beginner start weeks" every month, two months or six months so that there are not new dancers every week. (5) One useful trick is to only teach a couple of dances (for example rumba and foxtrot) and then when you move onto new dances (for example salsa and quickstep) that creates an opportunity to bring new dancers into the class (although they may still be behind in basic skills and transferable skills so it is not a perfect solution). Remember that if you do this you can still play the previous dances during social dancing at the end of the class to allow them to keep the skills going.

## My Favourite Format for an Evening of Classes and Dancing

7:30-8:15 Beginners Class. 8:15-8:45 Social Dancing. 8:45-9:30 Advanced Class. 9:30-10:30 Social Dancing. I always push very hard for people to join in the social dancing, otherwise I find they often skip it: For example, I ask my advanced dancers to come at 8:15 to dance with the beginners. I play slower music during the middle social dancing session so that beginners can join in and advanced dancers warm up. I will encourage keen beginners to sit and watch the advanced class and then join in the social dancing again at the end. Finally, I allow keen advanced students who understand the need to keep drilling the basics (as high end performers in most physical professions actually do, despite what many seem to think) to join in the beginner class for free as this helps the beginners and helps create social/community links between the classes.

# Lead-Follow is the Core of Partner Dancing

## Introduction

### Lead-Follow is Central to Partner Dancing

*(I think this is useful for almost all students.)*

I often use lead-follow ideas to help students that are struggling: For many problems I find the solution is in the lead-follow connection between the two dancers. I am going to talk about 7 beginner lead-follow issues: I think these are interesting whatever your level. Then I will talk about 5 advanced lead-follow issues which I would expect to become relevant after (on average) at least a year of learning: Perhaps don't read these if you are just starting out as they could confuse you.

Further Ideas: I often discuss one of these ideas per lesson with a group class.

## Beginner Lead-Follow Issues

### The Leader is in Charge

*(A simplification to help beginners.)*

There are lots of very complicated ways to explain lead-follow. And some slightly complicated ways. And some fairly brief ways. With a "first week" beginner group I prefer to say "the leader is in charge". It is really simple and means you can focus on the basics of the dance and get dancing! The things you learn in the first week are designed to work even if the lead-follow is messy: so relax and have fun!

Further Ideas: I am pretty insistent on this. If you study my lesson plans for the "first lessons" of any dance you should notice that leading mistakes are generally not going to be a problem. For example, in the latin dances, if the follower misses a change they can just join in after they notice which is fine.

### Be Patient as the Follower

*(Leading can be difficult to learn.)*

I remember when I first started dancing I would dance (for example) back basic in latin and get stuck because I kept missing the place to change to forward-and-back basic. I found the best dance partners at this stage were the patient ones who let me keep trying! I had a lot happening in my head including trying to stay in time, trying to spot when to change, then panicking and forgetting which direction to go, then getting it correct but realising I would have to anticipate it in advance because once the correct moment arrived I had to have already started leading. So many things to think about! And for me the breakthroughs in my dancing in the early weeks and months were with partners willing to give me the time to work at it.

Further Ideas: I have found this can be a big problem. I have had angry followers saying it is not fair. In particular I find the followers can gain competency and be ready to move onto the next thing in less than half the time of the leaders. This can be 5 minutes instead of 10 minutes or 5 weeks instead of 10 weeks. I will usually say to the followers that they are welcome to try leading for a change while the leaders catch up. Alternatively they can skip a week or more of my classes and then restart once the leaders have had time to catch up. I have also in the past run a weekly "leaders only" class with free entry for followers (by invitation only in some cases) willing to just be "props for practising" in order to push the leaders on faster.

### Lead as a Team

*(A learning option.)*

You could work as a team. If you are dancing latin you might dance back basic and talk to each other at the same time deciding what to do next and then let the leader actually lead the change. For initial learning, the follower might even say: "I think I can see when we need to change shall I try it a bit so you can get a feeling for it?"

Further Ideas: I am clear in class that this is a temporary thing which can be very effective if the leader wants a bit of help. The main exception is if I am teaching a couple private classes, perhaps for a wedding dance, in which case they will only be dancing together and I will be pragmatic as this is not intended for functional partner dancing in a social setting and allow the couple to do whatever works.

### Leaders Can Say What is Next

*(I still do this after many years of dancing.)*

I still do this now if I want to relax my partner or if for some reason the lead-follow is not working very well. I simply tell my partner what is next! I try to say it in a relaxed way to communicate the idea it is not urgent (otherwise I have found some followers panic and dive into it thinking they missed something). I usually say it just before making the lead, perhaps saying "I'm about to lead a spin turn", so that the lead is also there and I often find that after a while with the same partner the need to say it goes away.

Further Ideas: I am very keen on this and encourage it. I am aware of some fashions that include the idea this is "wrong" and also that "you should not speak on the dance floor". I rarely encounter these etiquette issues and if I do; Honestly, I usually find the dance to be fairly uncomfortable and don't dance with that person again.

### Timing

*(I am very relaxed about this.)*

I find some people cannot hear the beat. Often, if they stick at the classes for a few weeks or months they finally get it. However, in the meantime I encourage them to tell the person they are dancing with and ask them to help keep them in time.

Further Ideas: I have never found a magic way to solve this quickly. I know there are clapping exercises and similar which I do use (sometimes) but I still find that for people who can't hear the beat it can still take a long time. Also, my honest feeling is that the clapping-type exercises are not very effective (although they can feel fun and students can feel like they are being taught well as it can seem well intentioned) and in fact I much prefer to use "stop start" exercises instead (as these are more contextual).

### Improvise if Possible

*(The sooner the better in my opinion.)*

I can only speak from personal experience as I have not done a thorough scientific study. First a definition: improvised dancing is where you take cues from the music (or other things) and dance without using pre-planned patterns or routines. So, people I have observed learning to dance in an improvised way I find take much longer to learn but in the long term they can become amazing dancers that stand out on the dance floor and are truly incredible to dance with. People I have observed learning to dance using routines and simple patterns (such as do a new move every 4th bar) learn very quickly but only ever seem to become "competent" and "good" but never "great". My students who have insisted on not improvising at the start with the intention of "learning to improvise later" I have observed having a lot of trouble breaking of the habits they first learnt and I have rarely seen them succeed in this plan.

Further Ideas: I encourage the leader to feel the dance and simply let things happen: This can be difficult and I am fine with a leader using a pre-planned routine or pattern as long as they then work at changing it, varying it and/or moving on from it within a few minutes (or maybe a bit longer depending on the student). For the follower I recommend trying to "let go" and "not anticipate" to allow the leader more scope for improvisation: For example, if the follower is always falling backwards as the 1st beat of the bar starts it can hold back a beginner leader from trying something else such as bringing the follower forwards.

### These Rules Change as You Get Advanced

*(Just so you know.)*

When I am most enjoying my dancing I am barely sticking to any of these rules! I won't tell you why yet as it will be a distraction! Learn the basics and there is more to come including an enhanced role for the follower!

Further Ideas: I have seen many teachers who seem to think my beginner rules are actually the only rules. Perhaps they simply lack the experience to realise there is more to partner dancing? (I suspect this may often be the case, with students having started to teach very early on before they learnt more advanced skills themselves.) Perhaps they are simply fans of a "fashion" of partner dancing where the leading is simpler?

## Advanced Lead-Follow Issues

### Create Opportunities

*(Leaders can create an opportunity instead of lead.)*

I find this is very follower-dependent. The simplified idea is that the leader creates a space or removes a block (perhaps moving out of the way) so that the follower can choose something. The advanced idea which I do a lot is that I will position my partner to be balanced at the end of one bar of music and then just slowly start suggesting a direction of movement and let the follower go when they want and using the move they want: At that moment when they go I have to be a follower and move with them. (It is not necessarily at the end of one bar of music but I think that is the easiest way to understand it.) I find this is even relevant in ballroom where even in close hold you can let the follower determine certain elements of the movement. However, some followers do not seem to like being given responsibility for choosing things like this (although I usually find they are dictating things like step-length or certain elements of timing even if they don't realise) in which case I will try to lead more strongly: But sometimes I can't (it is not my person style to do so) and it might simply mean the follower and I have a clash of styles and cannot dance very well together which can happen sometimes.

Further Ideas: I have only ever managed to teach this idea in a "workshop" or "masterclass" type format with open-minded dancers. I do not know any standard exercises that help but I am happy to improvise a teaching approach depending on the group.

### 50/50

*(An equal share of leading and following.)*

Very occasionally I find a follower willing to lead half the dance. We will simply take control at random moments with whoever has the strongest feeling of what to do being the one who leads at any given time. If I find a follower willing to do this they often have to be patient as my following is often rusty and it might take a few dances to get it working smoothly. And if I dance with someone like this for many weeks we often end up dancing in such a way that we never really know who is leading and it all just happens: Those are some of the most magic dances for me.

Further Ideas: I would not include this in a standard class. However, I enjoy sharing these principles in more detail and I find it is possible to "masterclass" this by doing one or more demonstration dances (where I "think out loud" and try to make it work) while allowing a discussion to develop with the class.

### Let the Music Lead

*(Let go completely!)*

Very occasionally I manage to "let go" and allow the music to lead my dancing. When this happens I am not consciously planning anything and the movements just happen. I can only do this with a dance I know very well so that the basic step and timing still work because they are so instinctive. I usually find I can only do this with a very good follower who is patient as sometimes the music isn't doing much and so we dance very simply, perhaps just marking time with a very basic step for one or more bars.

Further Ideas: I might "masterclass" this as well.

**Overbalancing Trumps the Leading**

*(Leading is the fallback when I am dancing.)*

In reality, when I am dancing I only lead if the follower is not already overbalancing and creating a movement already. I have sometimes danced with someone and it has then leading has come up in conversation and I have said "I actually only led about two things in that entire dance". The underlying principle for me is: Why force a follower to move forwards into a turn (which I might have planned) if there is a (perhaps very subtle) overbalancing occurring to their right which can be used to make a much more natural movement that will still be a great move. If these overbalancings are common with a follower I often stop leading and instead start manipulating their balance by nudging them (which is maybe leading by another name but anyway it is definitely a very different form of leading) one or two beats before I would normally apply a lead to encourage the overbalancing to be in the direction I want.

Further Ideas: (1) Again, this is another thing I might "masterclass". (2) Leading one beat early is something I will do with very "lazy" followers and sometimes I have been able to make a dancer who is very average with other leaders look incredible when I use this trick.

**Let the Space on the Dance Floor be the Leader**

*(Leaders can use space so why not let other spaces lead instead?)*

If I am dancing I often allow the space on the dance floor to lead me. I then lead my partner as per usual. Perhaps I am dancing ballroom (moving anti-clockwise around the outside of the room) and the couple in front shape to start going into the corner: If there is space in front of them I could now accelerate and have a big space for an expansive/fast movement forwards! And so on. I am always looking around the floor and sometimes I might track the movement of 7 or 8 couples to try and predict where there will be a gap for a running move in quickstep for example: If you ever see me start a fast running move and quickly pull out of it the likely reason is I saw a gap but it got filled by someone else so I had to abort.

Further Ideas: This is a central tenet of many teaching approaches for Argentine tango. I actually first learnt it for competitions in order to manipulate my position to be nearer the judges. But now I mention it often, including to beginners, as I think awareness of the dance floor and other dancers helps the whole room dance better and also helps with awareness of people nearby to avoid collisions, etc.

# *Partner Dance Lead-Follow Practice*

There is a YouTube video https://youtu.be/RPuA2VJV8_I that fits with this lesson plan. The numbered sections of the video and this lesson plan match to make working with both easier. For most students I recommend watching the video and regularly pausing (and maybe rewinding) as you also read this lesson plan. However, depending on your learning style, you might develop a better approach for you. Note, the video is designed so you can join in using a smaller space such as your living room.

## Section A: Introduction

### 1. Lots of Example Exercises

*(These are example exercises and I recommend that you find what works for you.)*

If you find an exercise you like you I strongly suggest you pause the video and take your time trying it out. I would suggest that if you find one good exercise you work on it and then come back to this lesson another day to then find another exercise. Each exercise will give you new things to think about in your dancing and to get the full benefit you might want to give yourself time to reflect and work on what you have learnt.

Further Ideas: I probably use one of these exercises every 3 or 4 partner dance lessons I teach. I would rarely do an extended lesson looking at more than one of them. However, if doing a private lesson, particularly training a follower, I might use a few of them.

## Section B: Warm Up

### 2. Warm Up

*(I recommend that you choose one or more dances to warm up to first.)*

The lead follow exercises are all quite abstract. I suggest you first do a couple of dances to remind yourself how it feels to dance and warm up your body to help avoid injury. A warm up may also help you to get a feeling for what is more difficult to lead or follow so you can make better use of this lesson.

Further Ideas: If I were teaching a class I would definitely use a warm up so I could watch and get ideas for which exercises I thought would be most useful for the students in the room.

## Section C: New Skills

### 3. Symmetrical Arms

*(Dancing symmetrically with your partner.)*

If you keep your arms symmetrical it can help leading and following be more predictable. It is not necessary to have any other parts of your body symmetrical.

Further Ideas: (1) Some styles of dance will have set ways of leading certain things that do not require symmetry. This is obviously fine but what we are looking at here is a technique that helps a follower follow any other style of dancing without knowing it (as long as that style has logical leading).

### Bent Arms at the Elbow

*(This means you can react faster.)*

Keep your elbows at least slightly bent at all times. They can then act as a "shock absorber" as you dance helping you keep your balance. This also softens the reaction of the follower to a lead as their arms will naturally "cushion" the push of the initial lead making the dancing also smoother.

Further Ideas: Imagine the opposite, imagine you have your arms completely straight. In this case even the slightest movement from your partner's hands will mean your hand moves: That movement will transfer immediately to your shoulder and possibly knock you off balance or maybe cause you to push back hard and disrupt the connection with your partner.

### 4. Tin of Baked Beans

*(How to dance with the follower's hand on the shoulder.)*

If the follower's hand ends up on the leader's shoulder it is an opportunity. The movement of the hand can still lead the whole body. This means the leader can lead simply by moving their shoulder. By varying how fast the shoulder moves, this means the baked beans would stay on the shoulder (meaning the hand stays on and the follower moves with the follower) or the baked beans fall off (in which case the follower's hand falls off and the follower stops allowing themselves to be led by the shoulder).

Further Ideas: Depending on the style of dance the standard way of following when the hand is on the shoulder might vary. I have taught here what I have found is a fairly typical amount of pressure in many styles.

### 5. Tin of Baked Beans (More Throwing Detail)

*(More ideas about how to throw your hand.)*

We demonstrate some different ways to make a hand throw look good and bad.

Further Ideas: The biggest issue I find here is with dancers not thinking about the hand at all. They just let it fly around and do not visualise how it will look. Spending time talking about it like this can really help. A good teaching technique can be to go to the extremes so I might sometimes get everyone to do their hand in slow motion (prizes for the slowest) just to get a feeling for doing it differently.

### 6. Tin of Baked Beans (Final Thought)

*(A more practical explanation.)*

In more practical language: (1) The leader does not want the follower's hand glued to their shoulder never to move again for the rest of the dance. (2) The leader does want the follower's hand to stay on there until the leader decides it should be moved. (3) So the follower should leave the hand on the shoulder and make a reasonable effort to keep it there. (4) So the leader will have to make a fairly sharp movement which the follower will then interpret as "oh my hand should fall off the shoulder now".

Further Ideas: I would not always go on about it this much in class. However, I'm assuming the worst and explaining it as much as I might have to sometimes. I have had to justify this sometimes to experienced dancers who think I'm "mad". The thing is that a lot of work is done on the hand-hand contact (for example) and that is considered normal. If you can do similar detailed work with the hand-shoulder contact it is possible to do more intricate dancing. For example, a leader and follower who have only learnt to lead through the hands will keep having to return to a pretty obvious position so that the next thing can be led. I am instead (with the right partner) able to whirl through a series of improvised, complex moves which someone watching often cannot see how they were led.

### 7. Body Follows Hands

*(The followers body follows their hands.)*

A practical way to lead is for the leader to be able to move just the follower's hand and expect the rest of the body to follow. Imagine an alternative where you had to manipulate their whole body. Alternatively, if the follower did not follow then it could still be a great dance but the connection weakens and certain high intensity, fast or technical moves are no longer possible.

Further Ideas: This is generally the main idea that I talk about in class when discussing leading and following. I think that as long as this is what is happening in the dance it does not particularly matter what the hand pressure is or other technicalities.

### 8. Step With One Foot Then the Other

*(We step together but always with alternate feet.)*

If you step with the right foot then the next step must be with the left. If you step with the left the next step must be with the right. If one of you follows this rule but the other does not it can mess up the footwork. Sometimes the step may be very tiny or even on the spot in a dance like rumba or waltz on the third beat but because these dances have a regular pattern it works.

Further Ideas: As we get more advanced the leader may purposely add a step or remove a step so they are on a different foot. This makes other moves possible. For the moment we are not considering this possibility. Also note that we are not talking about making a weight change on the spot which does actually happen in some dances like rumba.

### 9. Latin Lead-Follow Exercise

*(The leader stands still and leads the follower.)*

You will see this demonstrated with a rumba/salsa stepping. I find this is difficult for the leader and the follower. For the leader it can be difficult to lead while you do not have your own stepping happening to remind you where you are in the dance. For a follower you have no clues from the movement of the leader and have to just follow the movement of your hand or hands.

Further Ideas: I mainly use this for private lessons with followers to develop their following.

### 10. Paper Pressure Exercise

*(Using two pieces of paper to test the amount of pressure in the hold.)*

Some pressure in the hold is typical in most forms of partner dancing. The leader and follower slightly press against each other. Beginners rarely have any pressure in the hold as there are too many other things to learn, although this can depend on the order of teaching. I prefer to delay the concept of pressure so students can get more instant progress without technicalities getting in the way. My personal experience is that the most experienced followers and leaders often use only very slight amounts of pressure because they have learnt to dance so subtly they don't need the pressure to be very strong.

### 11. Holding a Tray

*(If you imagine holding a tray it helps you follow accurately.)*

If you have an imaginary tray in front of you it forces your hands to stay still. We use this to make your whole body move.

Further Ideas: I have heard of teachers during private classes taping the follower's hands in place so they cannot move to have the same effect.

### 12. Dancing With a Balloon

*(Use a balloon to test if you are staying the same distance apart.)*

By dancing with a balloon between you it is a test of whether you stay the same distance apart. You must step with alternate feet or the exercise does not work very well (or at least I can't see how it would work well).

Further Ideas: This is a fun exercise for parties!

## Section D: Dance Naturally

There is no "dancing naturally" section for this lesson.

# A Course of Lessons in Ballroom Dancing

Ballroom dancing can mean many things. Depending on the country (or region) you dance in there might be simply a repeated basic step (perhaps thought of as a "country dance"), or a complex set of rules to follow or an improvised dance that only requires a few simple guidelines to be followed. This book looks at a relatively improvised version of ballroom that fits with most versions of ballroom you might meet. You will learn social versions of these dances with an emphasis on "slow stepping" as a safe way for beginners to join in at a social dance. Quickstep is taught as a faster version of foxtrot. Waltz is completely different as there are 3 beats to the bar.

3 ballroom dances are covered in this book:

Foxtrot

Quickstep

Waltz

# Learning Foxtrot (Ballroom)

With a slow rhythm foxtrot is a good dance to start with. There is time to think. Also, if you step, for example, a tenth of a second too late it might not be a problem but this could be confusing in something like quickstep which is much faster.

There are 3 lessons in this book covering foxtrot:
Foxtrot Complete Beginners (Slow Basic)
Foxtrot Complete Beginners (Slow Slow Quick Quick)
Foxtrot Beginners Leader Solo Practice

# Foxtrot Complete Beginners (Slow Basic) (Ballroom)

There is a YouTube video https://youtu.be/FL7xj8-OEUw that fits with this lesson plan. The numbered sections of the video and this lesson plan match to make working with both easier. For most students I recommend watching the video and regularly pausing (and maybe rewinding) as you also read this lesson plan. However, depending on your learning style, you might develop a better approach for you. Note, the video is designed so you can join in using a smaller space such as your living room.

Further Ideas: I find foxtrot is a very variable dance to teach in terms of how quickly people pick it up. This lesson plan could be too slow for some people and in a mixed-ability class where I didn't want to go any faster I might simply choose to move onto a different dance after a while. Students finding it easy will not get bored. Students finding it difficult would generally still be able to dance foxtrot safely in "open hold" so they already have a dance to enjoy.

## Section A: Introduction

### 1. Walking in Time is Fun and Easy

*(Ballroom dancing is like walking.)*

If you can walk you can dance! Learn to step in time with your partner around the edge of the room. To make it more exciting simply vary the length of the step and the feel of the stepping to fit the mood of the music.

Further Ideas: I think it is vital to get this across straight away: Dancing really is easy! It really is just walking with a few considerations for your partner and the people around you. Anything beyond this, in my opinion, is simply an "improvement" and not a "necessity".

### Stop-Start Exercises

*(A key way I teach.)*

Further Ideas: In a real life lesson I might have done more "stop-start" exercises near the start. In particular the forwards, backwards and on-the-spot walking I think would have benefited from it. The reason I use these exercises is that some new students will (for some reason) either not realise the importance of the timing or won't realise they are not in time. Stopping and starting again a few times is one of the most effective ways I have found to deal with this. The other very effective technique I use is simply telling the student that "it looks great but if you step in time with the beats it will help you dance with others and it is more fashionable". However, if a class is in time the stop-start exercises are not necessary (although can help for other reasons sometimes). Also note that if this is a fun beginners lesson I will let the occasional person finding it difficult carry on out of time as they are probably only at the lesson for an "experience" and why make that experience one of being endlessly corrected?

Foxtrot Difference: I find the simplicity of the foxtrot often means less stop-start exercises are needed compared to other dances for complete beginners.

# Section B: Warm Up

## 2. Step Naturally

*(Dance as you would walk.)*

Typically we land in our heel as we walk forwards and in the ball of our foot as we walk backwards. This is great for dancing too. If you do not walk like this I recommend simply dancing the way you walk as this presumably suits your body.

Further Ideas: (1) Many teachers will specifically train a student to step a certain way. The spirit of ticket2dance is to focus on making dancing musical, improvisational and comfortable with your partner. I do not like spend time on retraining the position of the feet. (2) This particular exercise I might extend a lot during a "real life" class. However, as I cannot monitor the student watching the video I have made it fairly short in the video lesson in case they are not staying in time. The next exercise gives me more control as a teacher to manage their timing. (3) Extensions of this exercise include sharing ideas of how different students walk, trying different music to learn to dance in time to different tempos and also hear the beat, experimenting with exaggerated stepping to let the body learn new ideas and practising keeping the head level while you step.

## 3. Turning Stepping into Dancing

*(Some structure is added to the stepping.)*

We practice dancing on-the-spot, forwards and backwards. Forwards is mainly for the leader. Backwards is mainly for the follower. On-the-spot is for leaders and followers perhaps when starting or for when there is an obstacle in the way on the dance floor.

Further Ideas: (1) Exaggerating like this can be useful for many students to see what would otherwise be too subtle to notice when learning a new skill. (2) I will almost never mention that the backwards steps are for the followers at this stage. Leaders do dance backwards eventually and I don't want them ignoring this skill. Also, I think talking about this is distracting when I can tell them later at a more useful moment.

# Section C: Skills

## 4. Stop-Start Practice

*(Practice the timing with some stop-starts.)*

Rather than spend ages talking about how the stepping works I find a stop-start exercise teaches the same thing without lots of teacher waffle!

Further Ideas: I love exercises that replace the need for the teacher to talk. If you really like the sound of your own voice why not talk at the same time as doing this exercise! Non-verbal learners have something to do while ignoring you!

## 5. Leaders Watch Behind Your Partner

*(As you dance round the room the follower is looking the wrong way.)*

It is up to the leader to watch where they are going to stop the follower hitting anything. Please be careful.

Further Ideas: I watch my groups carefully when they first start dancing and often decide I need to shout stop loudly to prevent a collision. Once I have done this once normally the reality (and considerable embarrassment) sinks in and the students are more careful. I prefer to do this "practical approach" rather than waffle on about it endlessly.

## 6. How to Stand With the Feet Offset

*(Position the feet slightly offset to help avoid collisions.)*

Simply picture the leader's feet either side of the follower's right foot.

Further Ideas: There are many ways of explaining this position but I like this particular approach as it seems really simple. I think you could argue that it might encourage the leader to point their toes inwards too much (assuming that is uncomfortable for them) but I will try to watch my students and mention it individually or to the whole class if it seems to be an issue.

### 7. The Leader Dances Forwards

*(If you are a leader face the direction you are going.)*

Leaders dance around the edge of the room side-on to the wall. Face the direction you are going and turn as you reach the corner.

Further Ideas: This seems obvious to an experienced dancer and also to many beginner students. However, I have found that making a big fuss of this really helps my students. Possibly the main benefit is that it creates an implied confidence in the students (that they are already doing the basics well) and means they are distracted from worrying about the steps and are already starting to be thinking more of the big picture.

### 8. Step on the Same Side

*(The follower and leader step on the same side.)*

When moving around the room the leader steps on the left foot as the follower steps with the right foot. And similarly on the other side. This means you can easily check your dancing by checking if you are stepping on the same side.

Further Ideas: This only works when the leader is going forwards and the follower backwards. Or when the leader is going backwards and the follower is going forwards. If, for example, they are standing side-by-side and going the same way this will no longer be the case. I am not discussing this here because it is a simple message for a complete beginner dancer and I don't think it is completely misleading as we are not saying that it is universally true. I find natural dancers are not usually confused later when this pattern changes.

### Closing the Feet

*(A hint of an advanced skill to work on later.)*

Notice that during this lesson I briefly say something like "maybe we close our feet together" as a throwaway line a couple of times. This is so that attentive learners will pick up on this and if someone already knows this skill they realise it is appropriate. However, for most students I am not highlighting it yet. Closing the feet between steps is a fantastic improvement that I encourage a lot in improver dancers and often cover in private lessons.

### 9. How to Dance Around the Room With the Feet Offset

*(Now dance around the room.)*

Use the same skill and start dancing around the edge of the room. Keep stopping and starting again if you need to.

Further Ideas: I like that at this point people can already dance safely at a social dance if they stick to the edge of the room doing this exercise.

### 10. How to Place the Feet

*(How should I place my feet? However you like!)*

Step in a way that is comfortable for you. We are dancing to be sociable and not to do things a particular way to win competitions for a given style of ballroom dancing.

Further Ideas: If you are teaching social dancing I strongly encourage you to let the students have natural body movements for them. Relearning how to move their bodies is a distraction from learning everything else and can even result in injury. I once had a teacher physically force my foot to an angle that nearly caused serious injury (I have out-turned feet and it is a strain to hold them facing directly forwards).

### 11. Close Hold

*(How to stand in close hold.)*

If you want to dance close step towards each other, hold hands on the leader's left side and on the right the leader puts the arm around the back of the follower and the follower puts their hand on the leader's shoulder.

Further Ideas: I will not even mention this if I don't have to. In general my students will just improvise and one of them often asks and I simply demonstrate and say something like "you can copy what I do if you like". This feels to me like something to sort out in more detail later and anyway in social dancing I have seen so many different ways of standing my experience is that it does not matter.

## 12. Dancing Closer Means Being More Careful

*(The feet are closer so watch out for collisions.)*

Dancing closer is traditional and looks and feels nice. It can make sharper turns and more dynamic lead/follow more possible. The cost is that we need to be more precise with our feet. This can take many weeks to start feeling comfortable enough to do for a whole dance without looking down.

Further Ideas: The reason this is taught sooner than in waltz is because we are simply stepping with one foot and then the other without the complication of sets of three steps. So, in foxtrot the beginner is ready to try something like this sooner.

## 13. Practice Exercise: Vary the Distance as You Dance

*(Dance around and vary the distance between you.)*

My students report this is very useful. I stumbled on this exercise once and now use it all the time. Dancing close is difficult but as a beginner it is normally ok to drift in and dance close for just a few seconds and then drift back out again. You can dance further apart and still enjoy foxtrot but most people set themselves the ambition of learning to dance closer.

Further Ideas: (1) This seems to be a good way of working on the stepping and timing without suddenly forcing the students to dance close. Rather than suddenly dancing in close hold students can build up to it and see the connections between the open and close hold as they practice. (2) This might seem early, especially as later there is more "free practice" dances. However, I find this is a good exercise to use early on as I find most people can dance foxtrot in "open hold" (when they are a long way apart) very easily and get bored of it very quickly. This exercise helps these bored students be more challenged early on.

## 14. Alternative Way to Start

*(You can do weight changes from side to side to start on opposite feet.)*

Doing weight changes from foot to foot and then stopping together means you are then ready to step on the same side. The leader should lead this and the follower just moves their weight across every time they feel the leader doing it. Preparing like this at the start of the dance means the leader could start with either the left or the right.

Further Ideas: I like to mention this even if a group is struggling (which would normally mean holding things back to simplify the learning) as I feel it is so important. I often find that it helps students understand better how the whole thing is supposed to work.

## 15. Moving the Upper Body

*(The movement of the upper body is optional. There are many good reasons to instead hold the upper body still.)*

A swinging motion with the upper body often makes the dance easier to learn at the start. I find beginners often find it makes the dance more fun as well. And in fact I find this movement tends to spontaneously appear in most classes even if I do not teach it: my theory is it is simply very obvious. Later on it can get in the way of leading and following. The movement can also start to get boring after a while. I strongly recommend you learn not to do it so that you are not stuck in the habit of always swinging the shoulders.

Further Ideas: (1) This is also important because many dancers do not like the upper body moving and think it is "wrong". I think it is sensible for beginners to practice not moving the shoulders so they can more easily social dance with people who like to hold the upper body still. Also, I find it really does get in the way of lead-follow in the more advanced moves. (2) However, I do this occasionally as a variation so have no problems with my students doing it sometimes as well.

## 16. Reminder of Feet

*(Reminder of who steps with which foot when.)*

The leader steps forward with the left as the follower steps back with the right. The leader steps forward with the right as the follower steps back with the left.

Further Ideas: This is in the video to recreate the moment in the class where some students ask: "Duncan this is all making sense now but can you just remind me the feet again".

### 17. Practice Time

*(Music to practice to.)*

Some individual practice time. If you like you can join in with me as I keep restarting. Restarting can be a great way to keep practising the important skill of starting and then dancing around the room. It also helps with the ability to recover on the dance floor if you lose the timing or if you have to stop for some reason.

Further Ideas: (1) I would not require all students to keep stopping and starting and instead allow them to do something else if it suited their personal learning better. So, why am I doing it? Because I want the "learning support" to be there for those who are struggling and the rest can probably manage fine on their own. (2) Notice this "free practice" dance is after 2 or 3 "theory points" have been addressed so the students have something to work on: I find this keeps the faster learners happy as then they always have new things to try. However, students who are struggling with the basics can simply ignore the more technical things and keep just trying to get dancing in time.

### 18. Stepping Forwards is Easier

*(Forwards is easier than backwards.)*

The leaders should remember that stepping forwards is easier. So, as a leader you might have to hold back a bit and your step might feel very easy. It can depend on you and your partner though.

Further Ideas: I think this is less true as you get more experienced but for beginners I find it is nearly always true. Hence I'm saying it in the beginners lesson without any further explanation to keep things simple.

### 19. Dealing With an Obstacle

*(How to deal with an obstacle.)*

You can simply (1) stop and start again when there is space or (2) keep dancing on the spot and continue forwards when there is space. If you look very carefully behind you (in case someone is overtaking you) you might carefully overtake if the obstacle is not moving. Always overtake towards the centre of the dance floor. Do not undertake!

Further Ideas: I did not use to teach this. A lot of teachers I have observed don't seem to do so. However, I have found it to be very effective but I am not completely sure why. The students already seem to know this intuitively. Perhaps this exercise is actually a disguised way of reinforcing the message about dancing around the edge of the room. And perhaps this is another exercise that implies a confidence in the student (because it sounds more technical) and so helps them gain confidence.

### 20. Leaders Step Smaller if Necessary

*(Leaders you should try to step in time.)*

For a leader to step in time they need to step on the beat. If the follower has not moved very far then you cannot step very far. Do not push the follower out of the way. Also, do not wait and step late as that messes with the timing of the dance.

Further Ideas: This is a common issue I have seen in my students.

## 21. Practice Time (Repeat)

*(More music to practice to.)*

More individual practice time. As usual join in or watch or do your own thing. At this point it is great if you can almost completely ignore me and just practice what you can remember from the lesson so far. Challenges for the follower can include stepping further to make the dance travel further. Challenges for the leader can include pretending to deal with obstacles. And remember to stay in time with the music. Experienced dancers often try to step very slightly late to make it feel nicer. Definitely try not to step before the beat.

Further Ideas: (1) I would not require all students to keep stopping and starting and instead allow them to do something else if it suited their personal learning better. (2) I am trying to step slightly after the beat but perhaps less than I normally would. This is so that the students can see the "long-term aim" of dancing slightly after the beat but it is close enough to the beat to be "easy to copy". (3) Does the practice time seem long? I spent a couple of years of my early teaching career endlessly surveying my students to see how long they wanted practice dances to be. I have since checked this every-so-often in case their answers were merely due to a quirk in my teaching. And it turns out most answers are between 3 and 5 minutes and that this answer has been consistent for many years. (4) It might seem early to have another practice dance but we've talked about a couple of technicalities (including a significant challenge of dealing with obstacles) and I find students are desperate for me to stop talking and give them a chance to practice at this point.

## 22. Leader Waits for the Follower to Step

*(When stepping into the follower the leader must wait.)*

When is the leader a follower? When the leader is travelling forwards they obviously have to wait for the follower before stepping. However, the leader is obviously initiating the step. Confusing? Your dancing was probably working before so don't let this confuse you. Mainly I have mentioned this in case you are having problems with the leader stepping on the followers feet which is often caused by this.

Further Ideas: This is a bit advanced but I find that briefly mentioning it can help some students and others can simply ignore it.

# Section D: Dance Naturally

## 23. Stop-Start Practice

*(I lead a practice dance where we stop and start together.)*

The ability to stop and start is a distinct skill. It is a useful skill as it prepares us to deal with obstacles on the dance floor. It also begins to develop the skill of knowing which foot you are on which is essential for many more advanced moves.

Further Ideas: I try to call the stop and start consistently. This way people who get to know my calling and can feel when the stop is coming. I will often make a deep breath just before calling it or start the word slowly so that they can hear it coming. Also, I try to say it at a good moment which is not so early people are not sure which step I mean and not so late that some people miss it. This is one of the aspects of teaching dance that I found most difficult to learn.

## 24. A Final Practice Dance

*(A chance to practice again if you are keen.)*

Dance around, work on the things you learnt in the lesson. You can see us dancing on the screen to remind you of some of the skills and see the timing.

Further Ideas: I realise this "breaks the rule" I established earlier of giving "free practice" after some new ideas have been introduced for the students to practice. However, the structure for this lesson is to have a "dancing naturally" section at the end. In a real-life class this "dancing naturally" dance might be delayed until the end of the class and therefore be a "recap" after the students have danced one or more other dances as well.

# Foxtrot Complete Beginners (Slow Slow Quick Quick) (Ballroom)

There is a YouTube video https://youtu.be/VnC26kZZEmc that fits with this lesson plan. The numbered sections of the video and this lesson plan match to make working with both easier. For most students I recommend watching the video and regularly pausing (and maybe rewinding) as you also read this lesson plan. However, depending on your learning style, you might develop a better approach for you. Note, the video is designed so you can join in using a smaller space such as your living room.

Once you have learnt "slow slow quick quick", you might want to change between it and the slow stepping. I find the easiest way to change from slows is to turn towards the wall and then start doing "slow slow quick quick". I find the easiest way to change from "slow slow quick quick" is to simply continue walking forwards slowly at that point in the pattern and then gently turn so you are dancing around the room.

Further Ideas: I think this has the least realistic video lesson to go with it. The video lesson just doesn't feel like how I teach this. I think the reason is that I don't like teaching moves like this but I feel forced to because I see it danced so much socially. Reasons I'm not keen on this include the fact it is 8 steps to a set pattern which feels like too many. I have taught quickstep completely differently with very strong students as a series of slows and then showed them how to improvise adding pairs of quicks in anywhere. This improvisational approach is actually how I dance with good followers and so mimics how I personally dance (and how I believe I see many other advanced dancers also dancing). I am intrigued to try and develop my own approach for teaching all students (much as I have developed unique approaches for other dancing skills) truly improvisational quickstep but it is one of the things I have not got around to!

Further Ideas: Perhaps one thing missing from this lesson plan, which I felt was too long already, is clarifying (1) the slight angles that you can dance the forwards and backwards sections on helping you progress faster around the room and (2) the slightly different length steps the leader and follower make as they fit around each other. I would usually address these two things as necessary and not make them a formal part of a lesson.

## Section A: Introduction

### 1. Slow Slow Quick Quick

*(Watch a brief demonstration while I talk about it.)*

This is a popular way for beginners to dance foxtrot. The steps are often called slow, slow, quick, quick. I like to call them very slow, very slow, slow, slow to emphasise that none of the steps are really that fast.

Further Ideas: With a repeating pattern like this I like to demonstrate at the start so students understand straight away approximately what the pattern looks like.

## Section B: Warm Up

### 2. Feet Positions

*(Brief reminder of comfortable foot positions.)*

This particular lesson can really test how well you are standing. Here is a recap of the way you can stand to avoid collisions during the dance.

Further Ideas: This is something I often talk about. Even at high levels this can often be improved and is often holding people back. If you are looking down it might legitimately be the leader checking which foot the follower is on or it might be the leader or the follower watching the movements of the feet to aid learning. In general in partner dancing I suggest the leader has more reason to look down as they are choosing what to do next and if they cannot feel what the follower is doing they might check to be safe. However, it should never be necessary to look down to see where your own feet are and as a leader if you are doing moves or styles of dancing you know well and can feel what the follower is doing then looking down is almost never necessary for most dancers I have taught.

### 3. Stepping Naturally

*(Step naturally for you.)*

You don't need to learn fancy ways of stepping. Just step the way you would normally do. For most people this means landing on the heel as they step forwards and landing on the front (or ball) of the foot as they step backwards.

Further Ideas: This is something I only mention if it looks like an issue. Probably it needs mentioning half the time. And if people have previous experience of learning dance they often ask as other ways of learning dance can require certain ways of stepping even if it feels awkward. For social partner dancing I encourage the footwork to be natural.

## Section C: New Skills

### 4. Join in or Watch

*(The slow-slow-quick-quick pattern is introduced. You can join in or just watch as I do it lots of times.)*

"Join in or watch" is a great way to learn. I keep doing the slow-slow-quick-quick foxtrot move and you can copy or just watch. Do what is best for your learning style. You can keep rewinding to watch this section again and again to get plenty of practice so it feels comfortable. In words the movement of each step is "forwards, forwards, sideways, close, backwards, backwards, sideways, close" and then it keeps repeating.

Further Ideas: In reality I am not moving forwards nor backwards but going at an angle to progress faster around the room. This I think is fairly obvious and I find most students do it without being told. If a student is struggling I will not talk about this with them as I have always found this makes it more difficult and confusing in such a case.

Further Ideas: I will judge a class and keep doing it again and again until everyone is comfortable. If some people struggle initially I will try to keep going and let them work at it on their own as in my experience the initial stage of learning works best if they can keep watching it and trying to join in. The reason I do a few repetitions in the video where I stop after a few steps is to deal with some learners who will keep going even if they have not got it (and obviously this is also to ensure the lesson works in a small room). Stopping and starting again forces learners who are bad at managing mistakes to keep practising the start without then continuing to do it wrong if they start wrongly. When teaching a group I use the start-stop approach if I can see people bad at managing their own learning getting it wrong. Alternatively, if a class is really struggling I might get them into couples sooner so that they have the extra visual aid of someone directly in front to copy.

### 5. Breaking Down the Individual Steps

*(I break down each step individually.)*

This is done clearly and quickly and if you want to you can keep replaying to see it more times. This will not suit all learning styles but generally I recommend watching it through anyway at least once as you might learn something useful.

Further Ideas: I would not use this in a group class if it looked like people understood the steps already. If only one or two people did not understand it I might go straight onto dancing together because within another minute or so it should be possible to give time for independent practice to music and then I can help them separately.

### 6. Practice Dancing Together (No Hands)

*(Demonstrations of how the leader and follower steps work together.)*

Lots of chance to watch and/or join in with the leader and follower dancing slow-slow-quick-quick together. For this exercise every time we start the leader goes forwards with the left and the follower goes backwards with the right. This is typical and also doing it the same each time makes it generally easier for beginners. Once you get more used to it you might start differently.

Further Ideas: Sometimes students are confused because in other dances they mirror what their partner does. In this case they are not mirroring but instead moving in the same direction. I find this is usually best explained by emphasising that it is not a mirror and demonstrating rather than having a confusing discussion about how it works in words.

### 7. Breaking Down the Individual Steps Together

*(I break down each step showing which foot is being used and where it goes.)*

This is done clearly and quickly and if you want to you can keep replaying to see it more times.

Further Ideas: When teaching a class I try not to break the steps down as for most I find watching and copying is enough. Depending on your perspective dancing can be considered as a series of linked positions or a continuous movement. My personal experience of teaching is that different students find different approaches work best for them. For those who think of it as a continuous movement seeing it broken down can be confusing.

### 8. The Direction of Travel is Sideways

*(Demonstration of the direction of travel.)*

The aim is for the leader to face the wall and travel sideways around the side of the room.

Further Ideas: My personal experience is that this is a good thing to clarify just before giving a free practice time so the students have a simple goal which means slower learners still feel the reward of genuine success. I honestly think that if you can work around the room facing the correct way (without drifting into the centre too much) then you have achieved a fantastic amount.

### 9. Practice

*(A chance to practice on your own.)*

Dance around the room and keep stopping and starting as necessary. You can watch us doing it on the screen but we are only there so you can copy our timing if necessary and be reminded of approximately what to do. Do not copy what we are doing exactly as you are supposed to be free dancing for this exercise.

Further Ideas: The feedback from my students is that they find the free practice sections of the class very useful. It is a chance to consolidate, practice, try new things and ask the teacher questions without feeling intimidated by the whole class.

### 10. Leader Feet Position

*(Offsetting your feet makes it much easier.)*

Colliding feet can be an issue when you start dancing. Making sure your feet are not directly opposite each other is a way to stop the feet and/or knees colliding.

Further Ideas: I have seen this taught many ways. I am sure there are other good ways to do it but I find encouraging the leader to fit their feet around the followers right foot is a memorable and practical way to cover this.

## 11. Practice Dancing Together (Holding Hands)

*(More demonstrations to copy.)*

Join in or watch again. As with all the "join in or watch" exercises, if you are just watching I suggest replaying this section until you are ready to join in and then join in before moving onto the next exercise.

Further Ideas: For video purposes I am doing lots of repetition of this. The reason is that it is a big jump to go from just doing slows to doing a repeated pattern of different steps like this. For most learners lots of practice is needed.

## 12. Practice Dance Around The Room

*(Face the wall and move sideways around the edge of the room together.)*

As we have seen in the lesson already many times, the basic step danced continuously moves sideways. To avoid banging into a wall we slowly turn as we reach each corner and therefore dance around the outside of the room. (If there are a few of you learning together look out for collisions and simply stopping and starting again is a good safety technique.)

Further Ideas: If the class has not done much other dancing I might spend time stopping and starting the class as a whole to initially stop them from banging into each other. Or I might just do a quick reminder to be careful before they start.

## 13. Follower Forward Step Can be Awkward

*(This is a common question.)*

Followers, the forward step can feel awkward sometimes. I recommend that you let the slow-slow-quick-quick timing flow and just keep stepping. Students report it starts to feel more natural after a while. (Although obviously stop and start again as usual if necessary.) One reason might be that the leader is not stepping back very far. Another reason might be that the follower is not being used to going forwards (towards their partner) and this can also mean not being used to the idea their partner will move out of the way for them.

Further Ideas: Some people are naturally chilled out and this is not a problem. Other people are naturally going to worry about things. And I commonly get asked about this. What might feel "awkward" or feel like the foot is in the "wrong place" seems to be something to do with this being a more unusual shape compared to other partner dance moves learnt by beginners. I find this is almost always a case of creating a problem where none exists and that the student needs to work through it.

## 14. Practice the Quicks

*(An exercise to make the quicks feel easier.)*

Repeat the quicks over and over again to let your body get a better feeling for them.

Further Ideas: This is also an optional fun move but here it is just an exercise. I have seen many teachers try to explain to a student how to do a small detail in the dance. However, I find beginners generally cannot see the detail as it is all so new. By using this repetitive exercise the skill of the quicks is now easier to learn.

## 15. Leaders Try Not to Reach on First Step

*(The first step for the leader should be clear but gentle.)*

On the first step forwards the follower is having to travel backwards possibly after a not-very-clear lead. This is quite difficult so as a leader it is good to be gentle and not too pushy on that first step. Followers with experience will learn to step stronger but this takes time.

Further Ideas: There are lots of technical skills that can make this work better. However, at this stage of learning it feels better to me to not get too bogged down in technicalities.

### 16. Followers Please Allow Mistakes

*(Try to let the dance flow.)*

This is true for everyone but in my experience with this particular lesson I find it is mainly an issue for followers. I think this is probably because this particular lesson is more difficult for the leader: The follower may not realise this and become impatient. The dance is not going to be perfect straight away. However, it often still works with mistakes so just try to keep going. For me a key thing is that probably three-quarters of what I now dance I only learnt because something went wrong and we carried on dancing and I realised I had just discovered a fun new thing to do. So, be open to new ideas including those that just happen spontaneously.

### 17. Practice Dance

*(Join Debbie and Andy in this practice session.)*

Try what you have learnt to music. Stop and start as you need to.

Further Ideas: As I am always saying, giving personal learning time means students can learn to dance away from the support of the teacher and also they develop the skills that will help them grow into the hobby better (and there will be many times they do not have the direct support of a teacher and if they have already learnt to work on their own these will be more positive experiences).

### 18. Steps Are in Groups of Four

*(This is a quick reminder.)*

Remember we are breaking the dance into groups of four steps. A slow, then a slow, then a quick and then a quick. And then repeat.

Further Ideas: Why do I have this brief scene? Because I find it is a useful reminder and many people seem to forget the underlying simplicity as we get deeper into skill work.

### 19. Turning to the Left Too Much

*(If you turn too much you can end up spiralling into the middle of the room.)*

If you are on a crowded dance floor it is important to stay to the edge as a beginner. This means going in a straight line down the side and only turning in the corner. An easy mistake to make is to turn too much and end up in the middle of the room. Stopping and starting again is a good option here to stay safe.

Further Ideas: This may not be an issue for a typical class in which case I would not mention this to avoid confusion.

### 20. Holding the Upper Body Still

*(Following can be difficult if the leader moves around too much.)*

This is partly personal preference. If the leader moves the upper body a lot it can make following more difficult. This is where feedback from the follower can be helpful: remember no one is right or wrong and instead it is about what works best for each person and learning to work with different dancers and compromising.

Further Ideas: My personal experience is that advanced followers are generally one of two types. Type one like a clear lead without too much noise and these followers are usually open to more different ways of dancing. Type two like more styling to be added but usually this means they have a more specific way of dancing (perhaps a particular named style or particular style taught by a certain teacher or organisation) which means they can predict what is going to happen (if the leader also dances the same style) and so lead-follow is less important.

### 21. Not Always Forwards Then Backwards

*(An example of where you might break from this pattern.)*

As people get more practice dancing they usually find they can start making up their own patterns. This can take a few weeks but it is exciting to start making up your own ideas and feel the potential for future improvements! Here is one example of where you can break from just doing forwards in backwards and do one of them repeatedly to move either forwards or backwards into a space.

Further Ideas: Some students will realise they can improvise without being told. Others will do it without realising. Because many students will take instructions very literally (which can be a good thing) I often say in a throw-away comment before I get to this point in the lesson that the pattern can be varied. Fast learners will pick up on this comment, slower learners will usually miss it and therefore not be confused.

### Dancing on the Spot

*(Also a fallback for slow-slow-quick-quick.)*

The ability to dance on the spot if an obstacle appears can be used when dancing slow-slow-quick-quick to pause while still dancing. You can then pick up again when the way is clear and start from anywhere you like in the pattern.

### 22. Optional Foot Lift When Travelling Backwards

*(It is an option to lift the toes as you step backwards.)*

In case you spotted this in the demonstrations (or are finding yourself doing it naturally) here is an issue relating to the foot as you step backwards. For a beginner this is not really important. I mention it here in case it crops up in your dancing or in case you have seen it in the demonstrations.

Further Ideas: Some teachers might bring this up with most beginners. I have found in my teaching that taking the attention of a beginner dancer into their toes can disrupt learning the timing and how to dance close to their partner without colliding, so I only mention it rarely (it is in the video and this lesson plan for completeness).

### 23. Length of Step When Stepping Sideways

*(The side step is different.)*

I recommend thinking of the side steps as different from the forwards and backwards steps. They can be a different length, or the same length, depending on how you personally dance. The side steps are done quickly and can be more difficult to reach sideways (your leg joints are optimised for forwards travel) and for most people that I have watched the side steps are much shorter.

Further Ideas: I'm being vague on purpose so that people still dance the way that feels comfortable for them.

### 24. Fully Slow Down After the Quicks

*(This is important.)*

I find that many students get "carried away". I know I do in my dancing when I'm having fun so it is not a criticism! However, after the quicks really slow down immediately. A common fault I see is that the next slow is stepped too soon. Wait after the two quicks (stepped sideways) and wait until the moment in the music to take the next slow.

Further Ideas: I recommend you really watch out for this. I find a logical explanation using the exact amount of time for each step rarely works. I think the reason is that somehow the human brain gets confused by the quicks and starts measuring the timing wrong. So, even though it is technically not true, I find it feels like there is an extended pause after the quicks and before the next slow. And generally my students report the same.

## Section D: Dance Naturally

### 25. Dance to a Whole Song

*(Enjoy a dance to a whole song.)*

Stop and start as you need to. Using everything you have learnt for a whole song is a great way of consolidating your learning. Keep stopping and starting if you need to. If you are doing well you might try to repeat this lesson but do it all in close hold as a further challenge.

Further Ideas: "Contextual learning" is where you learn something in the way you will actually use it. Have you ever learnt something and then faced with having to use it realised you can only really do the exercises the teacher gave you but not the whole thing? This is why a practice dance is a good idea and why I have spent years as a teacher developing lots of complicated ways of teaching my students but have eventually just thrown most of the techniques away to just "get my students really dancing straight away"!

# *Foxtrot Beginners Leader Solo Practice (Ballroom)*

There is a YouTube video https://youtu.be/M7HkllJprZw that fits with this lesson plan. The numbered sections of the video and this lesson plan match to make working with both easier. For most students I recommend watching the video and regularly pausing (and maybe rewinding) as you also read this lesson plan. However, depending on your learning style, you might develop a better approach for you. Note, the video is designed so you can join in using a smaller space such as your living room.

## Section A: Introduction

**1. Solo Practice**

*(This is a quick lesson.)*

As always you can repeat the lesson for more practice.

Further Ideas: I am really not keen on the slow-slow-quick-quick basic. However, it seems so popular socially that I feel I have to teach it.

## Section B: Warm Up

Perhaps this does not need a warm up as is a simple practice exercise (which is the kind of thing I might use as a warm up) and a quick discussion.

## Section C: Skills

**2. Slow Slow Quick Quick Practice**

*(Join in as we dance this four step basic.)*

This is the same as we did in the beginners lesson. I think that if you can feel confident with this pattern the dance becomes much easier as you can then have "spare brain processing power" to dedicate to thinking about other things as you dance.

Further Ideas: Partly I ran out of time to record more clips but in fact there is a reason I recorded this and nothing else and that is that I simply think this is the most important thing for the leader to practice on their own for beginners foxtrot.

**3. Which Way to Face?**

*(We have learnt two different ways to dance.)*

Which way do we face for the "slows" version? Which way do we face for the "slow-slow-quick-quick" version?

Further Ideas: This feels like a classic situation where many teachers will forget that to a beginner this is not obvious. When I ask this question in class to beginners it is generally a difficult one and people have to think about it. But they do usually work it out. That to me feels like a good question (not too easy and not too hard).

## Section D: Dance Naturally

This section is maybe not relevant for this short lesson.

# *Learning Quickstep (Ballroom)*

I very strongly recommend learning quickstep after foxtrot. This is one of the few things I have seen nearly every teacher agree on! Quickstep is fast which if you are learning means you do not have much "thinking time". If quickstep seems difficult even after a bit of practice I suggest returning to foxtrot and trying quickstep again a few days or weeks later.

There are 10 lessons in this book covering quickstep:
Quickstep Complete Beginners (Slow Basic)
Quickstep Complete Beginners (Slow Slow Quick Quick)
Quickstep Beginners Leader Solo Practice
All Slows in Quickstep covers an additional 7 lessons.

# Quickstep Complete Beginners (Slow Basic) (Ballroom)

There is a YouTube video https://youtu.be/zpf1VtZPFIQ that fits with this lesson plan. The numbered sections of the video and this lesson plan match to make working with both easier. For most students I recommend watching the video and regularly pausing (and maybe rewinding) as you also read this lesson plan. However, depending on your learning style, you might develop a better approach for you. Note, the video is designed so you can join in using a smaller space such as your living room.

## Section A: Introduction

### 1. Just Like Foxtrot Slow Basic

*(This lesson simply builds on foxtrot slow basic.)*

This lesson is designed to go after the "foxtrot slow basic" lesson. They are almost exactly the same dance but foxtrot is slower and so easier to learn. So, do this lesson after you have done the "foxtrot slow basic" lesson and once you are feeling comfortable with the foxtrot.

Further Ideas: I like to teach quickstep as sped-up foxtrot as it feels like more efficient use of a student's time to learn two dances in not much more time than it takes to learn one dance. There are technicalities which mean this is not exactly true but at this stage I feel it is a fair approximation.

## Section B: Warm Up

You could warm up with some foxtrot first.

## Section C: Skills

### 2. Stop Starts

*(Enjoy dancing to a whole song.)*

Settle into the basic step and keep dancing to get comfortable and help you remember it for when you go social dancing. Remember to stop and start again as much as you need to.

Further Ideas: Stop starts are really helpful for developing practical skills such as dealing with obstacles on the dance floor and losing the rhythm.

### 3. Faster Than Foxtrot

*(Yes we are dancing faster than with foxtrot.)*

Just to clarify: (1) Yes the rhythm of the music is faster in quickstep. (2) We step in time with the music. (3) So this means we are dancing faster in quickstep.

Further Ideas: It might seem obvious to you (if you are the teacher) but the way people relate to music varies and some people may simply not be aware of the underlying beat. I have talked to students about this and some people are, for example, so into the lyrics that they simply haven't ever listened to anything else in the music carefully before.

## Section D: Dance Naturally

### 4. Dance Continually to a Whole Song

*(Enjoy dancing to a whole song.)*

Settle into the basic step and keep dancing to get comfortable and help you remember it for when you go social dancing. Remember to stop and start again as much as you need to.

Further Ideas: I like to give practice time where students dance and practice on their own and I go around giving individual help. If you are a teacher, then depending on your existing teaching technique this might sound odd and might not work immediately. My advice is to think about places in the lesson where you would normally lead everyone to dance together and consider changing those to "practice time".

### 5. Dance Continually to a Whole Song (Repeat)

*(Enjoy dancing again.)*

Just one more dance!

# Quickstep Complete Beginners (Slow Slow Quick Quick) (Ballroom)

There is a YouTube video https://youtu.be/c_WI6ySxeb8 that fits with this lesson plan. The numbered sections of the video and this lesson plan match to make working with both easier. For most students I recommend watching the video and regularly pausing (and maybe rewinding) as you also read this lesson plan. However, depending on your learning style, you might develop a better approach for you. Note, the video is designed so you can join in using a smaller space such as your living room.

## Section A: Introduction

### 1. Do This After Learning the Same Move in Foxtrot

*(Be patient!)*

This is much easier to learn in foxtrot. I do not recommend doing this lesson until you have done the same lesson in foxtrot and have practised and are confident with the move.

Further Ideas: I have observed and tried many different techniques for learning the quick steps in quickstep. The approach of first learning it in foxtrot is in my experience the most effective one. If you learn this first in quickstep before foxtrot I find it looks much more skippy and often never calms down.

Further Ideas: If I had a very patient learner who was also very ambitious I would consider drilling the technique of the slows and quicks and the ability to feel which foot they are on as three different skills over and over. Once they had those three skills I think they could then do good improvised quickstep. I have taught a bit like this sometimes but never as the main approach for a whole class.

## Section B: Warm Up

### 2. Foxtrot Warm Up

*(Perhaps revise the foxtrot first.)*

You could warm up by repeating some or all of the foxtrot slow-slow-quick-quick lesson. Or you might just do one or more foxtrot practice dances.

Further Ideas: When teaching I might spend up to (or even more than) half the quickstep lesson dancing foxtrot as a way of getting beginners ready. Dancing fast gives little time for learners to think. So, many learning points for quickstep can be covered whilst dancing foxtrot.

## Section C: Skills

### 3. Practise Dancing Individually

*(The slow-slow-quick-quick pattern danced to quickstep music.)*

This is very fast so keep trying again as many times as you need to.

Further Ideas: I try to encourage my students to be patient. It is very tempting to learn quickstep as soon as possible as it is a popular dance but it is very fast and generally better learnt once a student is comfortable with the basics of foxtrot.

### 4. Practise Dancing Together (No Hands)

*(Dance to music full speed with no hands.)*

We stand offset so you can see us both on the screen. You might like to practice facing each other so you are already getting ready to dance together holding hands or in hold.

Further Ideas: This is the sort of thing where I see students make lots of mistakes for sometimes ten minutes. If the students are continually stopping and starting, sometimes watching and clearly trying different things I will usually just keep demonstrating. This gives them time to watch or copy. The only time I will usually intervene and be more bossy in my teaching is if I see people continually getting it wrong who are either not aware of it or are aware but clearly do not have the learning skills to do anything about it. If students need supporting typical techniques I will use are "stop start" exercises, dancing to slower music, stamping the steps out so we can hear them and maybe stepping out the steps one at a time.

### 5. The Direction of Travel is Sideways

*(The leader faces the wall and travels sideways around the outside of the room.)*

Leaders face the wall and followers face your partner. I recommend starting near the wall. Then leaders travel sideways, keep facing the wall and as you reach the corner keep dancing sideways and also turn gently as you dance to face the new wall. You can smoothly continue dancing around the corner and then carry on along the next wall and so on.

Further Ideas: (1) Just before giving a free practice session I have found that this is a useful thing to mention for many students. (2) In the video version I take over half a minute on this which might seem like a long time. However, I have found this is a big problem and worth an extended demonstration involving at least one or two corners to make it really clear. (3) I find corners are the biggest issue but instead of highlighting them directly I prefer to start with "dancing down the wall" which most people seem to understand and then extend this into "waiting for the corner" so the two skills feel more related.

### 6. Extended Practice Together

*(Now dance around the room together without copying me.)*

Do not copy me, simply use what you have learnt to dance around the room. The demonstration on the video is so you can look at it to remind you of things if necessary. Some people also find it useful to see what the timing is of the song.

Further Ideas: Free practice is generally considered to be an important component of learning. I have found an effective approach for dance teaching is to include plenty of free practice once the students have enough skills to do contextual, continual practice in couples. By contextual I mean that the students are practising a real thing they could use when dancing. By continual I mean they can keep going round the room for a whole song without stopping.

### 7. Quicks Repeated

*(A useful exercise to get a better feeling for the quicks.)*

The quicks can be difficult to learn. They only last for two steps and many beginners find they are always surprised or panicked and never have time to relax into them. This exercise involves starting to do quicks and then continuing to do them. It is a sort of shuffling movement to the side.

Further Ideas: This was a real breakthrough in my teaching when I worked this out. I am sure others have independently had the same idea but I have never seen it elsewhere. This one exercise solves what seems to be one of the biggest problems for learners in quickstep of getting relaxed knees during the quicks and therefore preventing bobbing up and down. As a bonus it generally seems to make the quicks easier which is how I now describe them to my students: "quick steps are easy lets do some specialised practice to hone our technique".

## 8. Dancing the Quicks Flat

*(An explanation of how the quicks look better if done flat.)*

Bobbing can be caused by many things. My experience is that it often comes from students not bending their knees. However, you have a lot to think about in your dancing already so if you find you are bobbing and it is difficult to stop I suggest not worrying about it for a while.

Further Ideas: My experience is that if a student is going to smooth out the bobbing they will do it fairly soon. If they bob a lot it seems to go naturally after a few weeks if I keep gently reminding them of the final aim.

## 9. Diagonal Demonstration

*(Dancing diagonally can make the dance more fun.)*

A demonstration of how the slow steps can be danced at an angle.

Further Ideas: (1) It is tempting to also introduce the leader stepping outside at this point. I prefer to introduce that separately so that the students are learning one skill at a time. (2) So, yes the leader can step outside. I actually don't do this myself in social dancing and rarely teach it. I think it is a technique for going faster and I enjoy dancing and generally do not like to rush so it doesn't feel relevant to me.

## 10. Diagonal Side Step Length

*(Overtaking during each sideways section is important to make the diagonal steps work.)*

At different points either the leader or the follower needs to take small steps to allow the other to overtake. This is fundamentally how it is possible to dance the forwards and backwards sections at an angle.

Further Ideas: (1) Some dancers will not be aware of the length of their steps. Exercises such as everyone working as a class (or maybe in pairs) and challenging each other to either take very small or very large steps can work for this issue. (2) Why didn't I mention this in foxtrot? Well, this is designed as a course of lessons and I liked the idea of introducing it later. I might teach this in foxtrot depending on the situation (time left in lesson, particular needs of the class, etc).

## 11. Challenging Stop and Starts (to Foxtrot)

*(We do stop and starts with some challenging starts.)*

By varying how we restart I have made this a more difficult stop start exercise. It is not part of the "dance naturally" section because it is that little bit more difficult.

Further Ideas: (1) I'm doing this to foxtrot because we just looked at angling the step and it is a chance to slow down and practice that skill. Also, in quickstep classes in general I often mix in foxtrot to give slower learning opportunities. (2) You can adjust this exercise to be more difficult by varying the restarts like this or just by doing more stops and/or restarting faster. (3) Why didn't I put this exercise in the foxtrot lesson? This was absolutely on purpose and because I find foxtrot is slow enough that in general students can get dancing without it. I find "stop start" exercises promote precision and accuracy in stepping which seems very relevant in this faster dance.

## Section D: Dance Naturally

## 12. Dance Continually to a Whole Song

*(Enjoy dancing to a whole song.)*

Settle into the basic step and keep dancing to get comfortable and help you remember it for when you go social dancing. Remember to stop and start again as much as you need to.

Further Ideas: (1) Individual practice time is where a teacher can go around giving individual help. (2) In a group class I often use a slower song at the end for individual practice. This helps to prevent students who are struggling from having a negative experience at the end of the class. I might then put on a fast song "for fun" at the end and maybe do a demonstration dance at the same time. Yes some students will be able to do it and that could be annoying for other students but I find there is already a sense that "Alex and Chris always seem to learn fast" (for example) and the other students have had to come to terms with this already.

# *Quickstep Beginners Leader Solo Practice (Ballroom)*

There is a YouTube video https://youtu.be/bKVHFPbvV8A that fits with this lesson plan. The numbered sections of the video and this lesson plan match to make working with both easier. For most students I recommend watching the video and regularly pausing (and maybe rewinding) as you also read this lesson plan. However, depending on your learning style, you might develop a better approach for you. Note, the video is designed so you can join in using a smaller space such as your living room.

## Section A: Introduction

### 1. Solo Leader Practice
*(Quick introduction.)*

This video is for beginner leaders. It is a chance to do solo practice without a partner.

Further Ideas: I like to have things like this in reserve in case I get mainly leaders turning up to a class.

## Section B: Warm Up

No particular warm up is recommended.

## Section C: Skills

### 2. Slow Slow Quick Quick Practice
*(A lot of repetition of the slow-slow-quick-quick pattern.)*

A number of different songs are used and for each repetition I try to talk a bit differently about the steps to create new bits of learning.

Further Ideas: I try to find lots of excuses to keep practising this in class so my students keep getting practice of the basics.

### 3. Slow Slow Quick Quick Broken Down
*(A slow analysis of the slow-slow-quick-quick stepping.)*

I begin with some full speed demonstrations where I find different ways to describe the steps. Then we break the steps down and walk them through together. Towards the end we start to speed up eventually reaching full speed.

Further Ideas: I would not talk this much in class unless a majority of students wanted it as I feel it is a bit slow. I have done it like this here because I think it is a good approach for a more in depth solo practice lesson.

### 4. Dancing with a Broom
*(If you don't have a partner handy you can practice with a broom.)*

The broom recreates the follower's front foot and gives you practice not crashing into your partner.

### 5. Lots of Quicks
*(Keep quicking to get used to the feel.)*

Quicks can be awkward so this exercise has been designed to give dedicated practice for this skill. We do it to music and keep doing quicks from one side to the other. We look at issues including trying to keep your head level (which avoids bobbing).

Further Ideas: I like this exercise and usually drop it in for just 30 seconds quick practice on a regular basis. Alternatively, if there are people doing a lot of bobbing as they do quicks we might do it more often.

## Section D: Dance Naturally

You can obviously keep practising these skills as much as you like. However, remember that your stepping needs to fit around your partner in the case of the "quick quick slow slow" pattern so I would be careful of "over practising" it on your own and getting stuck with one or more steps that don't work with a partner.

# All Slows in Quickstep (Ballroom)

I enjoy adding contrast to my dancing. I see professionals and show dancers doing the same. Sometimes fast, sometimes slow. Sometimes large steps, sometimes small (although show dancing often doesn't look good if done small as the audience can't see it). In dancing you have two options for varying tempo: speed up or slow down. So, in quickstep I like slowing down because it gives me a variety of options I can use with beginners and/or dancers with more limited mobility. I have developed a repertoire of options which I am often asked to teach. In fact, I find this difficult to teach but hopefully this set of lessons will give you some useful input for your dancing or teaching.

There are 7 lessons in this book covering this topic:
Quickstep Improvers All Slows Introduction
Quickstep Improvers Slow Stepping Offset and Promenade (All Slows)
Quickstep Improvers Pivot Turn Back on Left (All Slows)
Quickstep Improvers Pivot Turn Back on Right (All Slows)
Quickstep Improvers Pivot Turn Back on Both (All Slows)
Quickstep Improvers Follower Zig Zag (All Slows)
Quickstep Improvers Leader and Follower Zig Zag (All Slows)

# Quickstep Improvers All Slows Introduction (All Slows in Quickstep) (Ballroom)

There is a YouTube video https://youtu.be/4XR_98C2zIo that fits with this lesson plan. The numbered sections of the video and this lesson plan match to make working with both easier. For most students I recommend watching the video and regularly pausing (and maybe rewinding) as you also read this lesson plan. However, depending on your learning style, you might develop a better approach for you. Note, the video is designed so you can join in using a smaller space such as your living room.

I consider the demonstration dance in this lesson to be very "artificial" because I tried to show lots of different ways of dancing slow steps in quickstep. I think this makes the demonstration look a bit messy but used more sparingly I think this way of dancing is a great option to add to your dancing.

## Section A: Introduction

### 1. Dancing Slows

*(Slows can be used in quickstep.)*

The matching video shows a demonstration dance where I only dance with slows. I am a big fan of using slows in quickstep. I think the main reason is that it opens up (1) many more options with relatively little effort and (2) it gives me much more variety for interpreting the music. In general I think they are well-suited for beginners on a dance floor with plenty of space, but on a crowded dance floor I think they are typically an advanced-only move.

Further Ideas: I find that some people do not like the idea of dancing slows in quickstep. I would point to tempo changes and contrast as being typical parts of creative hobbies such as dancing. Some incredible art is done with just one or two colours but in general it is acceptable to use a variety of often contrasting colours to paint a picture. So, I think using contrasting tempos and shapes in your dancing is good as well.

# Quickstep Improvers Slow Stepping Offset and Promenade (All Slows in Quickstep) (Ballroom)

There is a YouTube video https://youtu.be/_EWyst8QbsU that fits with this lesson plan. The numbered sections of the video and this lesson plan match to make working with both easier. For most students I recommend watching the video and regularly pausing (and maybe rewinding) as you also read this lesson plan. However, depending on your learning style, you might develop a better approach for you. Note, the video is designed so you can join in using a smaller space such as your living room.

## Section A: Introduction

### 1. A Practical Move

*(Offset and promenade are variations within quickstep.)*

It can be helpful to easily switch between offset and promenade without having to do any fancy moves. Having a simple option gives you a fall-back if you are in a difficult situation on the dance floor and is also another easy option to add more variety to your dancing.

Further Ideas: I think this is more of a "practical" move than a "fun" move. Dancers who have learnt the basics often understand the problem of "getting stuck on the dance floor and not knowing what to do". I would explain this lesson as offering a solution to many dance floor problems. Also, a dance needs simpler moves to be building blocks to fit around the more complicated moves.

## Section B: Warm Up

### 2. Just Slows in Normal Position

*(Warmup with slows danced in normal position.)*

This is a good warmup. You probably did this a lot when you were first learning.

Further Ideas: I think this is an important first exercise. Many students enjoy the quicks so much they (and/or their muscle memory) completely forget how to dance all slows. This needs to feel natural so you can concentrate on the more complicated things to follow.

### 3. Offset Position Step Breakdown

*(The steps are briefly broken down.)*

The steps are briefly broken down to make them clearer. Then we look at how to change between facing and offset position. It is important to be decisive because you do not want to be halfway between the two positions or the leader might tread on the follower's feet.

### 4. Offset Practice Dance

*(Warmup with slows danced in an offset position.)*

Dancing offset can feel awkward. It is generally not as nice and I would not encourage it. However, it will often happen in the middle of a dance and it is a building-block to lead towards other moves. So here is a chance to practice this occasional skill.

Further Ideas: For some students I find it very important to explain that this is not a good move to do on purpose. It is only really an emergency move of last-resort or a building block for other moves.

## Section C: Skills

### 5. Promenade Step Breakdown

*(The steps in promenade are broken down individually.)*

Promenade can feel strange to begin with. Yes you really are both walking forwards next to each other!

Further Ideas: I have done this briefly in the video as someone watching can replay this and other sections to get extra practice. In a group class I might spend more time on this.

### 6. Promenade Practice Dance

*(Join in or watch as we dance in promenade.)*

Dancing in promenade position can be fun. It feels very different to many of the beginner moves so really adds variety.

Further Ideas: I have experience of teachers teaching promenade as something that happens for just one or two beats then is over. This seems a waste if it is the first time a student is learning it. I encourage you (if you are a teacher) to let the student have some fun: remember it may be boring for you (and might also feel boring because you are used to more complexity) but in my experience it is new and exciting for many students who like to just hold the position for a while as they pause in their dancing (copying the type of pause they see professional dancers do).

### 7. Offset into Promenade

*(Changing from offset into promenade on the leader's left.)*

Do this gently so the follower can step safely and not be forced into an awkward step. It is done as the leader steps with the left because the follower then has time to prepare for the awkward through-step that happens when the leader steps with the right. When stepping forward with the left the leader gently opens up the hold and encourages the follower to move into promenade position. The next step should then naturally be forwards for leader and follower stepping together. You must do this gently (unless you are a very advanced dancer).

Further Ideas: This is a rare occasion where I am stricter in my teaching. I like to get the students doing this correctly straight away as initiating this move when the leader steps with the left is so much more effective. I aim for this to be the first shape they experience and therefore for that to immediately start to feel natural. I feel that a self-learning or experimentation stage is not effective for this particular skill at the start.

### 8. Promenade into Offset

*(Changing from promenade into offset on the leader's left.)*

This also works well as the leader steps with the left.

### 9. Offset into Promenade (Repeat)

*(Changing from offset into promenade on the leader's left.)*

This exercise is a repeat from before.

Further Ideas: This repeat makes a "learning sandwich" where one skill is repeated each side of another to help a student see the links.

### 10. Turn Your Upper Body During Promenade

*(As with most partner dancing if you are slightly adjusting your body to help it feel natural this might be obvious already.)*

We look at how the upper body can reposition to make the forwards movement feel more natural.

Further Ideas: This is definitely optional. In a group class I would only cover it if it look like an issue some people needed help with.

### 11. Promenade Hand Position

*(The leader's left hand can be symmetrical or go across further to create a lead.)*

If the leader has their hand in the middle then this looks symmetrical and a follower is likely to guess what is happening. If a leader pushes their left hand further across this helps lead the follower to open out. There are arguments for both but I prefer the option where the leader pushes the hand further so that it is a clear lead.

Further Ideas: I find the non-symmetry of the hands in this move can be confusing as it breaks a previous rule. So, I like to take a little a little time to discuss it because for more "thoughtful learners" it could distract them or make them lose trust in the teacher.

### 12. Why Does Promenade Position Exist?

*(Promenade position is a solution for travelling sideways together.)*

We look at all the directions you could move as a couple and how promenade position is a nice solution to moving sideways.

Further Ideas: This is definitely optional. I have included it as I feel it helps explain promenade position and also helps students understand how it is just an option and what else they might do at similar moments in the dance. I am also introducing a learning approach I use a lot in my teaching which is "looking at the different options from a particular position".

### 13. A Sharper Transition Between Offset and Promenade is Possible

*(Sharper transitions are more advanced.)*

Sharper transitions/movements in dance are more dangerous because if your partner does not do the same thing at the same time you can twist the other person (perhaps straining the knee) or bang into them. So, I would only teach this to advanced students.

Further Ideas: Injuries do happen in dancing as with anything. My aim as a teacher is to minimise those injuries. I consider teaching fast movements too soon to be one of the most dangerous things so I avoid it.

## Section D: Dance Naturally

You can simply find some music to practice to.

# Quickstep Improvers Pivot Turn Back on Left (All Slows in Quickstep) (Ballroom)

There is a YouTube video https://youtu.be/VUizcXjywwg that fits with this lesson plan. The numbered sections of the video and this lesson plan match to make working with both easier. For most students I recommend watching the video and regularly pausing (and maybe rewinding) as you also read this lesson plan. However, depending on your learning style, you might develop a better approach for you. Note, the video is designed so you can join in using a smaller space such as your living room.

This is a fun move that I think is only safe to be done on a social dance floor by experienced dancers. I have included it as an improver move because it is fun, not too advanced and if you are dancing on an empty dance floor or with lots of space, with the follower also looking out for danger, it can be used.

## Section A: Introduction

### 1. Demonstration

*(Health and safety reminder.)*

Remember to lead gently, beware of getting dizzy and be careful if travelling backwards. As this move involves suddenly stopping you need to be very sure that, for example, no one is travelling close behind you who will crash into you when you stop.

Further Ideas: The dizzy issue might seem obvious but I find some people will continue even if they are getting dizzy.

## Section B: Warm Up

### 2. Just Forwards Recap

*(Warm up with some slow basic.)*

A good reason to do this warm up is that the timing in the rest of the lesson is going to be the same. Remember to stand with the leader's feet either side of the follower's right foot and stay in time with the music.

Further Ideas: Many students are impatient to learn new things. So, offering new material can help with motivation and by making it more fun make the learning more memorable. However, I am always looking for ways to incorporate drilling the basics into my lessons. A warmup is a great way to do this. Top performers in most fields continually hone the absolute simplest of skills to gain a competitive edge: I like to give my students the same chance to excel.

## Section C: Skills

### 3. Pivot Turn Back on Left Step Breakdown

*(A dynamic turn to change from leader backwards to forwards.)*

When the leader is stepping backwards they can block as they go back on either foot and then turn. In this case we look at the situation where the leader blocks as they go back on the left to then go forwards onto the right while beginning to turn.

Further Ideas: This is the type of move that different classes can experience very differently. If you are a teacher I recommend being ready to highlight whichever of the parts of the move are causing the most problems. Eventually the leader might be aiming to be able to improvise in the moment blocking with either the left or right once both options have been learnt to make the dancing more responsive/creative. I think that improvisation becomes more possible once the "muscle memory" is learnt at which point much faster decision making becomes possible (which might be intuitive decision making).

### 4. How Many Steps During the Turn?

*(Take as many steps as you need.)*

This is a quick demonstration and discussion about how you can take as many steps as you like to make the turn.

Further Ideas: This can be very important for some types of learner, particularly those who try to copy exactly what the teacher demonstrates. Some learners will take what a teacher says very literally due to the way they hear instructions and so can be legitimately confused until this issue is explained.

### 5. Practical Application When Avoiding a Collision

*(This move can be underturned.)*

A brief discussion about how the move might be more or less than 180 degrees. This might be for creative reasons perhaps to catch a particular moment in the dance as you start going forwards or perhaps to create a shape on the floor as you move. Alternatively this might be a practical choice to avoid an obstacle.

Further Ideas: This is definitely something I would mention to fast/keen learners. For those who are struggling this may or may not help. For some struggling with this move it can increase confusion. For others struggling it can give them the freedom they need to make it easier. I will try to use my judgement to decide whether or not to cover this issue with a given student/class.

### 6. Demonstration of Adding Extra Turns

*(Extra complete turns can be added.)*

If you are blocked in and cannot progress further around the dance floor you might continue turning for longer to give the space in front of you time to clear. Alternatively, if the dance floor is very empty you might have the freedom to do stuff like this without regard for other dancers. This is not taught in the video but instead I do three demonstrations and talk over them.

Further Ideas: (1) I think this is a very fun move and can give fast learners and/or physically fit dancers a way to extend themselves. If a student is ready for this (by which I mean has the basic skills to learn this fast) then usually little or no tuition is needed and they can do it straight away after some personal practice time. This is a good example of something I like to let the student work on and develop themselves: this develops dance problem-solving and self-learning skills. I find the leader is the key person who needs to be ready for this option as even a very inexperienced follower can usually follow a reasonable lead to keep turning. (2) Note that I think this move is sometimes a bad choice. For example, if there is a "sense of movement" to the music I think the delay this move can create can be a "jarring mismatch" and not look/feel good. So, if you (or the DJ at your social night) is choosing lots of up-tempo music this move might never be a good choice.

## Section 4: Dance Naturally

### 7. Dance Continually Explanation

*(A simple pattern you can repeat for a whole dance around the room to practice this new dancing option.)*

You start walking forwards, go straight into the corner, come out backwards, use a pivot turn to return to going forwards and repeat!

Further Ideas: This is very dependent on learning style. Some students do not like exercises like this as they may have already processed the pivot turn and found a good way to incorporate it into their dancing. If teaching a group class I would make it clear this is only an option and they can do their own thing if they like. In a final section of a lesson like this some students will not even do the move because they choose to practice something else instead that feels like the right thing for where they are with their learning and that is fine.

### 8. Dance Continually (Practice Dance)

*(Dance continually to music.)*

We demonstrate on the screen so you have company as you try to do the same sort of "continuous practice" of this move (or do your own, alternative practice).

# *Quickstep Improvers Pivot Turn Back on Right (All Slows in Quickstep) (Ballroom)*

There is a YouTube video https://youtu.be/ibz1FwMPXbI that fits with this lesson plan. The numbered sections of the video and this lesson plan match to make working with both easier. For most students I recommend watching the video and regularly pausing (and maybe rewinding) as you also read this lesson plan. However, depending on your learning style, you might develop a better approach for you. Note, the video is designed so you can join in using a smaller space such as your living room.

This skill is the same as the pivot turn back on the left but in the opposite direction and starting at a different point in your stepping. Learners who learn by shape or feel often do best leaving this until their pivot turn on the left is good. Learners who learn by thinking or understanding often do best by learning this at the same time so they can better analyse what is happening by comparing the differences and similarities.

## Section A: Introduction

### 1. Beware of Getting Dizzy
*(Health and safety reminder.)*

Keep the lead gentle, beware of getting dizzy and be careful when travelling backwards. As this move involves suddenly stopping you need to be very sure that, for example, no one is dancing along close behind you who will crash into you when you stop.

## Section B: Warm Up

You might do a warm up dance.

## Section C: Skills

### 2. Pivot Back on Right Step Detail
*(A dynamic turn to change from leader backwards to forwards.)*

As the leader is stepping backwards they can block as they go back on either foot and then turn. In this case we look at the situation where the leader blocks as they go back on the right to then go forwards onto the left while beginning to turn.

Further Ideas: This is the type of move that different classes can experience very differently. For teachers, I recommend being ready to highlight whichever of the parts of the move are causing the most problems.

### 3. How Many Steps to Turn Around?
*(Take as many steps as you need.)*

This is a quick demonstration and discussion about how you can take as many steps as you like to make the turn.

Further Ideas: This can be very important for some types of learner, particularly those who try to copy exactly what a teacher demonstrates. If you are a teacher be careful of always demonstrating the same and instead I try to vary my demonstrations to show that there is not a fixed way to dance it.

### Pivot Turn Back on Right is Less Useful

*(A discussion.)*

Stepping back on the left means you then turn clockwise. Turning clockwise sends you towards the centre and if you are in a corner makes the turn easy. Stepping back on the right means you turn anti-clockwise which sends you towards the wall which can be awkward and also makes corner turns more difficult.

On a social dance floor you are supposed to overtake away from the edge. An anti-clockwise turn does not set you up for an overtake of this type. This is another reason why the pivot turn back on the right is less useful.

Further Ideas: I talk about issues like this even with students that prefer to ignore things like this and just dance intuitively (although with students like this I'll obviously try to be brief). The reason I think this is important is because I find many students respond with "oh that explains why it felt odd I won't bother remembering this move". Helping them make the decision about which moves to retain in their repertoire is something a teacher can do to "add value".

### 4. Practice the Move

*(Some repeated practice.)*

We will do it together. I will add some discussion and help about when we can and cannot start the turn.

Further Ideas: It is very important to get used to only doing the move when you step back on the right. Depending on a student's other hobbies and skills the idea of doing something only on one side of the body may not be something they have previously done and in this case it can be very difficult to learn.

## Section D: Dance Naturally

### 5. Dance Continually Explanation

*(A simple pattern you can repeat for a whole dance around the room to practice this new dancing option.)*

You start walking forwards, go straight into the corner, come out backwards, use a pivot turn to return to going forwards, and repeat!

Further Ideas: This is very dependent on learning style. Some students do not like exercises like this as they may have already processed the pivot turn and found a good way to incorporate it into their dancing. If teaching a group class I would make it clear this is only an option and that you can do your own thing if you like. In a final section of a lesson like this some students will not even do the move because they choose to practice something else instead that feels like the right thing for where they are with their learning and that is fine.

### 6. Dance Continually

*(A song to do the continual exercise to.)*

Do the exercise we just talked about to a song.

Further Ideas: In a real life class I would put the music on, let people do this on their own and I would go around helping. With beginners I might start dancing for the first half a minute just to remind the students what they are aiming for.

# Quickstep Improvers Pivot Turn Back on Both (All Slows in Quickstep) (Ballroom)

There is a YouTube video https://youtu.be/t1uzovcD0U0 that fits with this lesson plan. The numbered sections of the video and this lesson plan match to make working with both easier. For most students I recommend watching the video and regularly pausing (and maybe rewinding) as you also read this lesson plan. However, depending on your learning style, you might develop a better approach for you. Note, the video is designed so you can join in using a smaller space such as your living room.

## Section A: Introduction

### 1. Do the Other Two Lessons First

*(This lesson follows on from previous learning.)*

This lesson is designed to be done after the "Pivot Turn Back on the Right" and "Pivot Turn Back on the Left". I would recommend doing both of them more than once and getting plenty of practice before trying this.

Further Ideas: If my students are quick learners or good at coping with problems in learning I might try this very soon and see if it works. If it doesn't my students have then at least got a feeling for what they are aiming for. With a more "fragile" class I would hold back so they do not get the disappointment of failing.

## Section B: Warm Up

I would suggest that you warm up for this lesson by doing one or more exercises from the "Pivot Turn Back on the Right" and "Pivot Turn Back on the Left" lessons.

## Section C: Skills

### 2. Is the Pivot Turn Back on Left or Right Better in a Corner?

*(If you are able to time the move you can choose which foot to block with. We look at choosing the better side for a corner.)*

A pivot turn back on the left means you make it round the corner sooner. A pivot turn back on the right can be more fun as it takes longer to get round extending the move.

Further Ideas: (1) I try hard in my teaching to create choices for students rather than tell them what is best. Dancing is often described as an art form and in that case it seems reasonable to allow people to have different, subjective choices about how they dance. (2) However, in this case I would recommend usually turning the quicker way if the dance floor is crowded so that you do not create a "traffic jam".

### 3. Which Way to Pivot Challenge

*(We keep blocking on different feet and then working out which way to turn.)*

Depending on which foot we block on we turn a different way. If the leader blocks when stepping onto the right the turn will be anti-clockwise. If the leader blocks when stepping onto the left the turn will be clockwise.

Further Ideas: This can be very difficult. Some students may not have experience of feeling a different choice of movement for each side of the body. This can depend on the skills they bring from other hobbies and activities. I have seen teachers get very frustrated with students, even accusing them of not listening. It is possible for the idea of a side-dependent movement to be so strange that they just do not understand however hard they try to listen. Please be nice if you are a teacher! In this case I often leave it and come back to it another time and maybe also work on other side-specific skills elsewhere in the lessons to try to develop the general skill.

### 4. Which Way to Pivot Challenge (Without Stopping)

*(As before but we keep stepping.)*

This gives very little time to work out what to do!

Further Ideas: Again, this can be very difficult. I might return to this every week for five minutes for a couple of months to let it slowly develop in a class setting.

## Section D: Dance Naturally

### 5. Knowing Which Way to Turn (Done Fast)

*(The same continuous exercise as in previous videos.)*

This is the same as the continuous dancing practice in the "Pivot Turn Back on Right" and "Pivot Turn Back on Left" videos. The only difference is that the leader is challenged to vary the foot they block with as they step back before the pivot turn.

Further Ideas: I consider this to be a more technical, advanced move. So, if I was teaching advanced students I would likely give them practice time. With a class more recently moving onto advanced things I would still give the practice time but be ready to take over again and return to "guided" or "supported" practice.

# Quickstep Improvers Follower Zig Zag (All Slows in Quickstep) (Ballroom)

There is a YouTube video https://youtu.be/i9oCGPj_mU8 that fits with this lesson plan. The numbered sections of the video and this lesson plan match to make working with both easier. For most students I recommend watching the video and regularly pausing (and maybe rewinding) as you also read this lesson plan. However, depending on your learning style, you might develop a better approach for you. Note, the video is designed so you can join in using a smaller space such as your living room.

This lesson is designed to work best after the Slow Stepping Offset and Promenade lesson.

## Section A: Introduction

**1. Keep Trying Again**

*(This lesson is designed for you to retry sections.)*

This video does not repeat the move over and over during "guided practice" type exercises. This is unusual compared to the other video lessons in this series. The reason is I decided to demonstrate and teach it in a line so it would work well in a video and that means we cannot keep repeating without going "out of shot". I would expect the typical student to have to retry this 10 or more times because of the slight limitations imposed by the video.

Further Ideas: Even in a real life class this can be difficult. If the room is large enough I might get everyone lined up at one end of the room so we can do a few repeats before reaching the other side. However, a free practice dance where I come around helping (with students dancing around the dance floor anti-clockwise as usual) generally works for me.

**2. Demonstration**

*(A demonstration quickstep dance just using this move.)*

A zig zag can be a fun move. I would try not to overdo it but could do it as an extended variation even for 16 bars sometimes. As you get more advanced you can vary the timing of the slow stepped moves and sometimes do them half time or double time.

Further Ideas: I find that some people do not like this move. Sometimes I can talk them round by suggesting it is good practice to get used to stepping through which is a useful skill for following many other moves. But this "improvisational slows" style in quickstep does not suit everyone.

**3. Beware of the Arms**

*(Leaders watch out.)*

As a leader it is easy to accidentally push your partner around with your arms. This move has a focus on the feet and involves twists. So, it is easy to start doing strange things with the arms. Followers please give feedback if something feels painful or wrong. In my experience the most likely problem with this move is the leader pushing their arms around oddly and perhaps too strongly. However, do not assume this is the problem as it could be something else: I recommend working together and "problem solving" to try to fix it.

Further Ideas: I often find in partner dancing that when something is not working well, the "mistake" can turn out to be the oddest thing and often is not the "obvious" thing. For example, if a leader seems to be pushing a follower it might be because: (1) The follower is not actually following and resists too much. (2) The leader is leading at the wrong time meaning the follower cannot follow so has to resist or fall over. (3) The leader is leading exactly on the beat and ideally it should be just a brief moment of time earlier so the follower has warning. (4) The follower is missing a step so ends up on the wrong foot.

## Section B: Warm Up

### 4. Just Slows in Normal Position

*(Warmup with slows danced in normal position.)*

This is a good warmup. I am guessing that you probably did this a lot when you were first learning.

Further Ideas: I think this is an important first exercise. Many students enjoy the quicks so much that they (and/or their muscle memory) completely forget how to dance all slows. This needs to feel natural so they can concentrate on the more complicated things that are about to be covered in this lesson.

## Section C: Skills

### 5. Stepping Offset

*(We will learn this from offset position.)*

So, this seems easy but it is setting up the line we will dance along and how the basic dance looks before the zig zag is added.

Further Ideas: If I am going to keep using a particular space to teach I will generally try to show where I will be dancing with a demonstration of something obvious first. This can help students "understand the space" and be able to relate the new moves to previous things they have learnt.

### 6. Demonstration

*(What it looks like.)*

This is what we are aiming for. We will be breaking it down and learning the separate bits first.

Further Ideas: I generally find most dance teachers understand demonstrating the whole thing first. Some students don't like to see it but they can always look away. Other learning styles really benefit from seeing the whole thing first.

### 7. Leader Steps Walk Through

*(The leader steps are broken down.)*

The leader does not have much to do!

Further Ideas: I find it very important to emphasise that the leader is doing nothing different. This helps stop the leaders from trying to do anything else. It also helps the followers understand that they cannot look down and mirror the leader.

### 8. Follower Steps Walk Through

*(The follower steps are broken down.)*

The follower steps involve sometimes stepping forwards, backwards and also slightly sideways.

Further Ideas: This is a rare occasion where I am stricter in my teaching. I like to get the students doing this correctly straight away as initiating this move when the leader steps with the left is so effective. I aim for this to be the first shape they experience and therefore for that to immediately start to feel natural. My experience is that a self-learning or experimentation stage is not effective for this particular skill at the start.

### 9. Leader and Follower Together

*(We practice together and I call the leader steps.)*

We now practice together and I call the steps of the leader as we go through. We do two basic steps (for example the leader steps with the left and the right, making two steps) and then go straight into doing the zig-zag. If this is confusing, "part 11" of this lesson might work better for you.

Further Ideas: A viewer can keep rewinding as required. If I am teaching a class then I try to judge how much practice is required and might ask people if they want to practice on their own yet.

### 10. Leader and Follower Together (Repeat)

*(We practice together and I call the follower steps.)*

We now practice together and I call the steps of the follower as we go through. Similarly, we do two basic steps and then go straight into doing the zig-zag.

### Very Slight Up-And-Down Lead

*(Yes I am doing that.)*

To make the lead clearer I tend to rise slightly (bringing my follower up with me) when they need to make a twist. I find this encourages them onto the balls of their feet (which for most people seems to make a twist easier and safer) and also I find it "traps" the follower (if you are up slightly you cannot move so far) helping them be receptive to a spinning or twisting lead.

Further Ideas: (1) I might not mention this depending on the students in a particular class. (2) I have met some other teachers who teach the same principle and others who believe it is wrong! It seems to work for me (and I find it a powerfully effective lead technique for dancing with strangers in a social setting) so I like to teach it.

### 11. Changing from Offset Walking to Zig Zag

*(It is good to learn how to initiate dancing zig zags.)*

The change can work best if done as the leader steps forward with the left because this gives a whole beat to prepare the follower before they have to take the unusual forwards step.

Further Ideas: If we start using a regular number of steps before the change I remind students that this is just an example.

### 12. Changing from Zig Zag to Offset Walking

*(You need to learn how to exit from zig zags if you want to use them socially.)*

This is fairly easy because two of the zig zag steps are just walking anyway. So, then you can just carry on walking.

Further Ideas: I think this generally feels easy for students. However, the leader has to give a clear shape with their upper body to show that the zig zags are not happening any more.

## Section D: Dance Naturally

I recommend that you find some music to practice to.

# Quickstep Improvers Leader and Follower Zig Zag (All Slows in Quickstep) (Ballroom)

There is a YouTube video https://youtu.be/9PTErtt2ldA that fits with this lesson plan. The numbered sections of the video and this lesson plan match to make working with both easier. For most students I recommend watching the video and regularly pausing (and maybe rewinding) as you also read this lesson plan. However, depending on your learning style, you might develop a better approach for you. Note, the video is designed so you can join in using a smaller space such as your living room.

Further Ideas: This is intended as a short extension lesson particularly following on from the quickstep improver video "Follower Zig Zag". Many of the same exercises and teaching points are also relevant here, however many students will find this easier once they have done the "Follower Zig Zag" lesson.

## Section A: Introduction

### 1. This is a an Outline Lesson Only

*(This follows on from another lesson.)*

This is an incomplete lesson plan designed to work after the "Follower Zig Zag" lesson if you are willing to work things out for yourself a bit.

Further Ideas: I will sometimes throw in complete new things like this in a lesson for a couple of minutes. It is a chance for fast learners to gain something new to keep them busy, for example they might be trying bonus material during free practice of things they found easy. I find other class members understand that "oh Chris is a fast learner" and don't resent that some students picked up extra content from the class.

## Section B: Warm Up

You might enjoy one or more dances as a warm up.

## Section C: Skills

### 2. Short Demonstration

*(A quick demonstration.)*

The leader zig zags at the same time as the follower zig zags. This requires doing a lot of things at once so can be very difficult and not necessarily worth the effort of learning if you find it difficult.

### 3. Changing from Offset to Leader and Follower Zig Zag

*(Change between the two moves.)*

We step through an easy place to make the change.

### 4. Changing from Leader and Follower Zig Zag to Offset

*(Change between the two moves.)*

We step through an easy place to make the change.

## Section D: Dance Naturally

I recommend that you find some music to practice to.

# Learning Waltz (Ballroom)

I like to be very clear with my students: Waltz is very different from foxtrot and quickstep! There are some similar skills but I think the best way to learn waltz is to have a clear mind and "start fresh" with your learning. There are three beats to the bar and we step on each beat. This creates some fairly complicated patterns. Luckily we do not have to understand the patterns, and as long as we follow a few simple rules (step in time being the main one) I generally find that it works really well.

I would say the improvers and advanced lessons I have included are a bit of an "odd bag". However, I thought through my choice of lessons to include carefully and they are some of my favourite things to teach.

I have included the curved basic because I find that this one "little tweak" to the basic means I can enjoy dancing a basic step for a lot of the dance without getting bored: The only proviso is that the follower step is slightly stretched for this move so I try not to curve too far.

The 360 degree turns are similar to what a lot of other teachers cover and I think they give a great option for beginners. The way I teach them, these turns are fairly self-contained and do not "leave you in an awkward position" afterwards.

You might be wondering why I teach 360 degree turns. The reason is that I find it is easier for students to understand than "end up facing this (teacher demonstrates) way compared to the way you were facing before". Yes it can be more difficult to get all the way around but the good news is that we then cover that in the lessons as well.

There are 12 lessons in this book covering waltz:
Waltz Complete Beginners
Waltz Beginners Dancing Closer
Waltz Beginners Solo Practice
Waltz Beginners Solo Practice (Extra Exercises for Leader)
Waltz Improvers 360 Turn to the Right
Waltz Improvers 360 Turn to the Left
Waltz Improvers 360 Turn Both Ways
Waltz Improvers All Forwards
Waltz Improvers Curved Basic
Waltz Improvers Leader Backwards
Waltz Improvers Leader Curve Backwards
Waltz Advanced Using Rumba as Variation

# Waltz Complete Beginners (Ballroom)

There is a YouTube video https://youtu.be/vVGeyhYoULM that fits with this lesson plan. The numbered sections of the video and this lesson plan match to make working with both easier. For most students I recommend watching the video and regularly pausing (and maybe rewinding) as you also read this lesson plan. However, depending on your learning style, you might develop a better approach for you. Note, the video is designed so you can join in using a smaller space such as your living room.

## Section A: Introduction

### 1. The Beats Are in Sets of Three

*(I generally see students who keep stopping and starting again do best.)*

I see big smiles from students as they learn waltz, which I often discover is because they like the music. I personally also love the rhythm and movement it creates. I so like the basic step I am happy just dancing that socially even though I have a wide variety of other things I could do. For many people the timing initially feels odd but I strongly recommend sticking with waltz for a while and everyone I have ever taught finds it gets easier with time.

Further Ideas: I nearly always see students finding waltz awkward initially but then enjoying it after a bit of effort. Unlike foxtrot we cannot simply start by "walking" because of the way the dance is split into sets of 3 steps. Because we cannot simply "turn walking into dancing" I find it takes a little longer to get going in the lesson.

## Section B: Warm Up

### 2. Stepping in Time on the Spot

*(Get started by stepping in time with the music on the spot.)*

It is good to learn one thing at a time. The first thing we introduce is stepping with the music. In theory most people are already used to walking on the spot so the timing is the only new skill. However, if you have an old injury, or for some other reason find stepping on the spot awkward, you might find this initial exercise needs replaying a few times to make it easier. As usual, you can choose whether to join in or watch depending on what works for your learning.

Further Ideas: For learning from a video I encourage people to keep trying to copy this exercise until it works. However if I am teaching someone and I am in the same room and they are finding it difficult I might dance with them so they can see and feel what it should be like and maybe learn it quicker. If I help someone directly like this I try to resist the temptation to keep talking to them as they often just want time to work on it without a sense of being rushed.

### 3. Alternate the Feet

*(The first step of each bar is stepped with alternating feet.)*

This is a great way of checking your stepping is good. Fundamentally it happens because there are 3 beats in a bar but you only have 2 legs. It is similar to the issue in latin dances such as rumba and salsa.

Further Ideas: In a private or group class I will usually just cover this if it looks like a student needs it.

### 4. Stepping in Time on the Spot (Repeat)

*(A repeat to really get used to the basics of the waltz.)*

If you can step comfortably in time you are halfway there. I continually emphasise the first beat because it is so important. Once we start moving around the room we will be moving forwards on different feet each bar and I find that this is much easier (and so saves time in the long run) if we do the stepping on the spot more.

Further Ideas: Some students get impatient. However, if we do not get really comfortable with the timing I find that the dancing can look laboured.

### 5. Stepping on the Spot (Individual Steps)

*(Each step is broken down individually.)*

In case it suits your learning style a quick look at the stepping broken down.

Further Ideas: In a private or group class I will usually just do this if it looks like a student needs it.

### 6. Stepping in Time on the Spot (Second Repeat)

*(Once more for luck!)*

We keep trying to make it feel more natural and easy.

Further Ideas: I sometimes use 10 or more songs and quickly do 10 to 30 seconds from each one. The main reason I have not done this in the video is due to the cost of getting copyright clearance for that many songs.

## Section C: New Skills

### 7. Stepping Forwards on the First Beat

*(The movement comes mainly during the first step.)*

We start dancing on the spot and then introduce a forwards movement on the first beat of every bar. This forwards movement will be on alternating feet because of the three beats to every bar.

Further Ideas: Obviously the followers will be moving backwards. However, they will sometimes have to move forwards in later moves. I find there is a benefit to having the whole class together during these initial exercises. Also, if people go on to practice at home it can be useful for the follower to be familiar with the leader steps as well (as this helps students be able to support and help each other).

### 8. Stepping Forwards on the First Beat (Round the Room)

*(A chance to practice to a new song and this time keep going round the room.)*

This does not have stop-starts so is appropriate for a repeat exercise where you are already starting to get the hang of it.

Further Ideas: I try to vary the music as much as possible during the lesson. If we just learn to one song there is a danger the muscle memory will be stuck going at one speed. I am never completely sure if it is best to learn in a straight line or going round the edge of the room. This is why I usually do both with a class. They seem to each suit different learning styles.

### 9. Stepping Backwards on the First Beat

*(This is what the follower will be doing straight away and what the leader will eventually have to do in some other moves.)*

Exactly the same ideas apply as before but moving backwards instead of forwards on the first beat of the bar. Obviously be careful as you cannot see behind you as easily as you can in front of you.

Further Ideas: If a class is finding waltz particularly difficult I might do this exercise with the leaders travelling forwards in a group in front of the followers travelling backwards. This means there is less need to talk about who is doing which steps and the learning can be more visual and less abstract.

### 10. Step Naturally

*(Simply step the way you would normally and generally it should all work out well.)*

If you step forwards you usually land on the heel of the foot then gently settle into the whole foot. If you step backwards you usually land on the front of the foot then gently settle into the whole foot. If you walk on the spot I encourage you to do whatever feels natural.

Followers you might notice some dancers "releasing their toe" as they step backwards but you do not need to do this. If you do it naturally anyway that is a bonus as it is considered in many styles of ballroom to be good technique.

And to emphasise, do not try to copy the teacher too much! Stepping is an individual thing that is partly dependent on your body and personal style. Yes there are some "universal things" that most people dancing waltz will do. But no not everyone has to look exactly the same. (Note I am talking about social dancing and not competition dancing where sometimes there are more strict rules.)

### The Balls of the Feet

*(Having your weight forwards.)*

As we move onto more advanced dancing it is almost universal in all dances I have seen to have the weight in the front of the foot. However, for absolute beginners I do not even like to teach this skill because I think it is another distraction from getting started and can easily be sorted later (as long as it is not left too long, perhaps mentioning it in the second lesson). If I see a student with the weight in the ball of the foot I might compliment them on it and tell them individually to keep that as it will be useful later but also remind them to step into the heel when going forwards.

### 11. Starting to Dance Together

*(The position we stand in and getting started.)*

We look at how to stand and how to start.

Further Ideas: I believe starting is a skill. If you are just starting the concentration needed to work out how to stand and get started is generally high and it seems unreasonable to me to expect a student to then just be able to keep dancing after concentrating so hard on such a difficult task. This is why in my lessons dancing together for an extended period is a separate exercise. I like that this gives separate "success points" where the students can feel good about what they have learnt.

### 12. The Direction of Travel is Forwards

*(The leader travels forwards around the edge of the room.)*

In a typical social setting you are looking to dance around the edge of the room. There will generally be almost no space between you and the wall or the carpet so that the more advanced dancers have plenty of room in the centre. Obviously you can be more flexible if the dance floor is very quiet.

Further Ideas: I find this is worth clarifying at this point so that students know what to do during free practice.

### 13. Practice Dancing Together

*(An extended period to practice dancing together.)*

Use what you have already learnt and keep practising. Stop and start again every time you start getting overwhelmed, every time it just feels wrong or just when you want a breather.

Further Ideas: (1) Something that I emphasise here is the need to stop and start again. Even if there is just a vague feeling something is wrong stopping and starting again might fix it. (2) Obviously if the dance floor only has beginners then not everyone needs to be on the outside of the dance floor. In this case I will often go around encouraging faster learners (or simply people who step further) to move towards the inside of the dance floor.

### 14. Practice Dancing Together

*(Another chance to practice.)*

A second chance to dance in open hold working on the timing and so on.

Further Ideas: There is a theory in teaching that you should give students a focus for their practice to make it more effective. In this case I have broken that rule as I feel this is a key point to keep trying to make all the things we have talked about already work in real dancing.

### 15. Stop and Start Practice

*(Dance with me and stop with me.)*

This is a great way to develop your general skills. There will often be disruptions as you dance such as just making a slight mistake, people getting in the way, chatting to those around you or perhaps brushing against another dancer. Being able to stop and restart helps you deal with situations like this.

Further Ideas: (1) I try to stop and start in a consistent way for the whole exercise to make it easier for the students. It can be tempting to keep adjusting how I call it but I have found it better to be consistent and the students soon work out how to interpret what I say. I try to call before the moment they need to stop/start to give the students time to process the instruction. (2) Notice this is a more chilled-out stop-start exercise (compared to latin) which is because the stepping is fairly slow (and so I am trying to encourage a gentleness to the stopping to reflect that) and I'm also aware of waltz being awkward for beginners so I am trying to keep the learning environment more relaxed.

### 16. Stepping Back With Left and Right

*(Try to step back the same with each foot.)*

Warning: This is talking about the step backwards on the first beat of the bar. To clarify, you make 3 steps every bar in the music and we are looking at the first step only. To clarify, we are not measuring the second and third steps of the bar.

Some people favour one foot when stepping backwards. This can make leading awkward as the leader would then need to lead you differently depending on which foot you are on. So, try to make each foot respond the same in the dance.

Further Ideas: The difference between the first and the other steps is a form of "asymmetry" and similar issues can occur throughout partner dancing.

### 17. Stepping Backwards is Difficult

*(Stepping backwards is generally more difficult than stepping forwards.)*

The leader should remember that stepping back is not easy. Usually the person stepping forwards needs to hold back and not step too far.

Further Ideas: This is often obvious but I think it can still be good to talk. For example, some followers will take this as a challenge to step further which can be a good thing. We are not talking about it here but the step length should vary depending on if something is in the way. The reason I do not talk about it is because there is plenty of emphasis elsewhere in the lesson about stepping on the spot or going slowly if there is an obstacle.

### 18. Lead by Indicating

*(How to give a strong lead while not stepping forwards too strongly.)*

This is related to the previous learning point because warned not to go too far, some leaders begin to hold back and then find the follower does not move much either. So this is a good time to mention that leaders can give a gentle early movement to "indicate" or "telegraph" the next step. In any case this is a useful skill (although fairly advanced) for all dancers. Benefits include: (1) Collisions are less likely because the follower can move out of the way before the leader moves. (2) Followers have more notice so following is easier, less urgent and most followers I have met enjoy it more this way.

Further Ideas: This is getting very subtle. In many classes I would probably only deal with this only when it came up as an issue (perhaps this might come up after a few weeks). However, for completeness and to make this lesson as effective as possible for as many people as possible I have included it.

### 19. Feet Position for Close Hold

*(Offset your feet to be safer as you dance closer.)*

If you position your feet to be offset then collisions are less likely. Leaders can imagine their feet going either side of the follower's right foot. Followers just need to step consistently and let the leader fit around what they are doing.

Further Ideas: I find it can take a few weeks for students to get used to doing this without looking down.

### 20. Dance Close and Far Apart

*(An exercise where we keep changing from close to open hold.)*

This is optional: You do not have to do this. Some people are keen to get to dancing in closer hold sooner and others happen to find it fairly easy and want a chance to practice it. However, you might just use this song for another practice dance instead.

Notice how the leader moves in closer while dropping the right arm to go very slightly around the followers back. This is a chance to work at the close hold for a few seconds at a time. Dance offset to make this work without treading on each other's feet. Generally my students like this exercise and find it to be very effective. It is fine to look down while you do this as it helps with the initial learning. Eventually you do not want to be looking down.

Further Ideas: I find most students are happy in open hold for the first lesson. Dancing close is quite difficult and a good thing to work on more in a second lesson or some other time. I have included it here as on balance it feels worth including as an option for this learning resource.

### 21. Spot the Mistake

*(Can you see the deliberate mistake?)*

Challenge: Watch carefully. I probably make lots of mistakes but one of them in particular I am trying to make. Congratulations if you notice more!

Answer: I start going too fast. I start off in time with the music but start going too fast. I think if you are dancing safely this is not a mistake (you can still enjoy your dancing) but most people say that dancing in time is more enjoyable once they get the hang of it.

Further Ideas: I have learnt through experience to always flag up that I will make other mistakes as well the one mistake I am trying to do. I like to mention this so students know to keep looking even if they have found one. I have found learners who like to follow instructions very carefully prefer this question precision.

### 22. Forward-Close-Close or Forward-Forward-Close?

*(Answer is either or neither!)*

You may not understand this. If your dancing is working then I don't think it is important. So you could ignore it.

Question: The leader steps forward on the first step. Generally the leader steps "on the spot" or a "close" on the third step. But, does the leader also step forwards on the second step?

Answer: I usually see people dance somewhere between the two where the second step is a smaller forward step. However, I definitely do both in my social dancing depending on the music and other things.

Further Ideas: (1) I am addressing this in the video because some people ask. If no one asks at this stage I will not mention it. I might mention it in a later lesson to help people develop more advanced skills and/or improve their body awareness during dancing. (2) Note this is not a "binary choice" between only the two options and there are other possibilities as well. For example with certain followers I regularly dance all three steps forwards (although the first step is usually longer).

### 23. Leader Left Follower Right

*(A pattern within the dance.)*

When the leader steps with their left, the follower steps with their right. And vice versa. Or you might think of it as both stepping "on the same side".

Further Ideas: Again I am addressing this in this lesson in case it is useful for some students. It is a particular issue that can hold some students up who like to think about feet. I would often save technicalities like this for later lessons if teaching a "real life" class. This is why I have tried to make it seem like a "throwaway" little thing in this lesson and not a big deal.

### 24. Dealing With Speed on The Dance Floor

*(Small steps or stepping on the spot is a way to deal with the traffic on the dance floor moving slowly.)*

If you are social dancing and the dancers in front of you are moving slowly then as a beginner you can simply take smaller steps to go slower. If the traffic is very slow you can even use your "dance on the spot" skills to wait for a while but still keep dancing.

Further Ideas: This can feel obvious and I usually see a group class realise this automatically during free practice. However, this has been included for people learning in small groups or in couples who do not have the "contextual learning" of being on a crowded dance floor.

## Section D: Dance Naturally

### 25. Stop Starts

*(Dance Waltz with me and join in with stops and starts.)*

We will keep starting, then stopping so we can start again. This helps to gain more awareness of the individual steps. It also develops the ability to deal with problems in the dance.

Further Ideas: An additional benefit of "stop start" exercises I find is that it is a way of controlling the learning of the group if the individual practice sessions are not working perfectly. I think they are (for the same type of reason) good for a self-learning resource as I cannot see the students and it helps me guide the learning more using the design of the exercise.

### 26. Practice Time

*(Enjoy a dance!)*

Practice and enjoy dancing to a whole song. Get really comfortable with the basic so you can remember what you have learnt and continue enjoying dancing waltz. If you want to learn more advanced things then getting confident with the basics is a great start. Remember to stop and start any time you need to.

Further Ideas: I often pretend I have something to get out of my bag or something to write down at the start of an individual practice like this. Many students will see that you are not looking and feel less pressure as a result. It can also help to stop the teacher from jumping in too early with help (if they are not looking they won't see the mistakes and so the students have time to do some learning on their own (and often will fix it themselves and gain confidence and other skills from doing so).

# Waltz Beginners Dancing Closer (Ballroom)

There is a YouTube video https://youtu.be/g66Immad50w that fits with this lesson plan. The numbered sections of the video and this lesson plan match to make working with both easier. For most students I recommend watching the video and regularly pausing (and maybe rewinding) as you also read this lesson plan. However, depending on your learning style, you might develop a better approach for you. Note, the video is designed so you can join in using a smaller space such as your living room.

## Section A: Introduction

### 1. Different People Like Different Holds

*(There are open holds, close holds and other types of hold.)*

Dancing is a creative hobby. We get to express ourselves to the music. I believe we should all be allowed to find our own ways to dance. For many, dancing in a close hold is better. Obviously as you are dancing as a couple you both need to be comfortable with the hold.

Further Ideas: If you have only learnt from a few other teachers you might think certain holds are better. My personal experience from watching and/or learning with hundreds of other teachers is that most people have their favourite way to dance and that it is important to let others find what works for them. I have seen local areas where everyone teaches the same and a perception develops that this is the only way to dance. And yet if you travel you can easily find whole countries full of people dancing completely differently.

## Section B: Warm Up

There is no warm up section for this lesson. You might simply enjoy a practice waltz to a song before doing this lesson. If the practice dance is difficult, perhaps try one or more dances to warm up some more: If it is still difficult perhaps it is best to do the complete beginners lesson again first.

## Section C: Skills

### 2. Feet Position

*(The leader's feet tuck each side of the follower's right foot.)*

This is a repeat of the exercise from the complete beginner lesson. The position of the leaders feet is shown in this section of the video. It is done standing still and you can copy. Notice that we are not talking about the position "forwards and backwards", instead it is the "left and right" position of the feet that is important.

Further Ideas: There are many ways of thinking about and teaching feet position. I like this approach because it is easy to remember (by which I mean it is memorable for the students).

### 3. Dance Together Thinking About the Feet

*(Now dance around the room thinking about the feet.)*

This is a first chance to practise getting the feet tidied up so that it is then possible to dance closer.

Further Ideas: It is tempting to do lots more technical explanations before giving the students a chance to practice. While the teacher may be impatient to share their knowledge the student's are still trying to understand the basics of this new idea and in my experience they want some time to practice before learning more technicalities.

### 4. Feet Position While Dancing

*(When dancing the foot position looks and feels different when stepping with the left and right feet.)*

When standing still the leader's and follower's feet will not be touching. When the leader steps forward with the left, the follower's right foot moves as well which means they remain apart. When the leader steps forward with the right, the follower's right foot does not move which means they can become close and maybe even brush against each other.

Further Ideas: I often do not like breaking down movements like this because I find it is too technical for beginners. However, for beginner waltz it is particularly important because I find that the use of alternating feet on the first beat of each bar makes stepping with the wrong foot a common mistake, meaning collisions are much more likely than in foxtrot or quickstep.

### 5. Practice Dancing Together Closer

*(A chance to try dancing closer.)*

As the feet get neatly positioned to avoid leg/knee/feet collisions it becomes possible to dance closer. Time to have a go! Keep retrying this as many times as you like as this is a typical place for people to want extra practice.

Further Ideas: (1) I have tried so many ways to teach this and avoid collisions. The conclusion I have come to is that they will happen. So I just remind people to be gentle and not get too ambitious. More sensitive leaders may go through an extended phase of stepping forward tentatively and my experience is that this passes naturally after a while as long as I remind them about the aim to step more strongly when they feel ready. (2) I feel there is a strong culture in many parts of the partner dancing community which says dancing in close hold is best. My personal experience is that I enjoy open and close hold. Some say that leading and following is easier in close hold. My personal experience is that very accurate leading and following can still be done in open hold but that the skills required are slightly different.

### 6. Practice Dancing in Close Hold (Optional)

*(Note that dancing this close can make it tempting to take smaller steps.)*

You will probably find yourself taking smaller steps in close hold. I think this is fine and natural. After a few days or weeks or months of dancing in close hold many people learn to stretch into longer steps and often it is possible to eventually step further because the lead-follow is working around a tighter turning circle than in close hold.

Further Ideas: I am mentioning this because it is a relatively common issue for beginners in my classes.

### 7. Turning in Open and Close Hold

*(Sharper turns are possible in close hold.)*

This is a practical demonstration of the difference between turning in open and close hold. This is a long term benefit of learning to dance closer and might not work for you yet.

Further Ideas: I consider this to be a "long term benefit". In a private class where I can carefully guide the learning this benefit might appear within half an hour. In group classes it might be a few weeks before I address it.

### 8. Leader Steps Slightly After the Follower

*(The leader creates an opportunity to step but the follower actually takes the step.)*

This is quite advanced but becomes important now we are dancing closer. If your dancing is already working and you are not doing this then I suggest not worrying about this too much. A lot of leaders will do this naturally anyway as pushing into a step regardless of what the follower is doing can intuitively feel wrong.

Further Ideas: This is complicated as it is beginning to really look at how the follower and leader can be dancing fractionally out of time with each other. I have met many teachers who never seem to mention this and my suspicion is that many teachers do not know about it. The difference in timing can vary from move to move but in this particular case when I am leading I will step slightly after the follower but it will barely be noticeable if you watch.

### 9. Role of Upper Body When Turning a Corner

*(The upper body can be used by the leader to suggest a direction.)*

Now that we are dancing closer and have the potential to turn more sharply we can use the upper body to make the lead clearer. As a beginner I think it is fine to just tell your partner what you are planning to do, but if you can start leading with your body it can be definitely make it more fun and it creates the potential for more fluid and improvisational dancing.

### Reminder of Feet Closeness Sideways and Forwards

*(Something I often cover many times in a class.)*

In a typical "real life" class where someone is not rewinding a video and managing their own learning more I think I have always had to repeat the feet position message again.

### Giving the Student Choice

*(Flexible teaching to make group classes more student-focussed.)*

It is possible to spend a lot of time making the hold closer and closer to make more advanced moves possible. However, I prefer to create an environment where the close hold is seen as optional. Some people like to dance further apart and some people like to dance close. However, those that like to dance apart often do not like dancing close so it seems better to mainly teach a more open hold and make the close hold optional.

## Section D: Dance Naturally

You could simply choose one or more songs for free practice. I recommend: (1) Looking down every-so-often to check how the feet look. (2) Looking up at other times as you get more comfortable. (3) Sometimes stopping and holding your position and then analysing it.

# *Waltz Beginners Solo Practice (Ballroom)*

There is a YouTube video https://youtu.be/Y_LZqDE_7KU that fits with this lesson plan. The numbered sections of the video and this lesson plan match to make working with both easier. For most students I recommend watching the video and regularly pausing (and maybe rewinding) as you also read this lesson plan. However, depending on your learning style, you might develop a better approach for you. Note, the video is designed so you can join in using a smaller space such as your living room.

## Section A: Introduction

### 1. Practice on Your Own
*(A chance to do extra practice.)*

If you are keen to do extra practice but don't have a partner handy you can use this lesson. If you have a partner you could also simply dance individually and do this lesson for extra practice.

### 2. For Leaders and Followers
*(We will do leader and follower steps in this video which are generally identical.)*

I feel waltz only needs one solo practice lesson plan. Leaders and followers are generally doing the same types of thing.

Further Ideas: If I am teaching a group class I often use leader steps when teaching everyone. The main reason is that in general I find leaders find the lessons more difficult at beginner level. There could be many reasons but my theory is that it is mainly because the leader has to make more decisions during the dance and having to think in advance simply makes it more difficult.

## Section B: Warm Up

This section is empty. I recommend you use the complete beginners lesson as a warm up or simply go straight to section 3.

## Section C: Skills

### 3. Forwards on the One
*(Dance with me going forwards on the first beat of every bar.)*

Practice stepping forwards on the first beat of every bar. The fundamental skill in waltz is being able to start each bar on alternating feet. This will eventually feel natural and doing extra practice like this, even if it starts to feel boring, will give you a great foundation to build from. Remember you can join in or watch.

Further Ideas: In more advanced moves you will not always be alternating. It is typical to learn a skill with some basic rules as a framework and then later learn to break those rules. An alternative approach is to learn to be very disciplined and continually take one step at a time always with the next foot. I like this alternative approach but generally do not use it with beginners because I find that for many it takes much longer to learn (arguably some never get it but this is never seen by teachers as these people give up and quietly never come back). So, in waltz I like to cover the skill of stepping alternately later as an improver or advanced thing instead.

Further Ideas: The leader benefits from having a strong sense of where the first beat of every bar is. The waltz has three beats to the bar and dancing in a way that is sympathetic to this rhythm is something I have seen in all versions of waltz. Some of my comments in the video relate to this and are trying to nurture this sense in my students.

### 4. Forwards on the One (Repeat)

*(We repeat the exercise.)*

Same exercise, new song.

Further Ideas: In waltz the pattern of a nearly identical movement which includes a pause and starts on alternating feet is relatively complex compared to other dances. I try to project calm and confidence to my students and say things like "this is great progress we're on the way" and "we keep getting better every time" to remind them they are improving.

### 5. Forwards on the One (Second Repeat)

*(We repeat the exercise.)*

Same exercise, another new song.

Further Ideas: This is being repeated a lot because I find my students generally want a lot of practice of the waltz basic step. Also, I find providing different songs can help. Why is waltz beginners generally more difficult? I think it is the alternating feet; My evidence for this is that by far the most common mistake I see is to go forwards on the wrong foot.

### 6. Backwards on the One

*(Similar to the forwards exercise.)*

Practice the basic waltz stepping but going backwards instead of forwards.

Further Ideas: I have put more emphasis on going forwards as the confidence of the leader to drive the dance forwards is fundamental to making the dance work as a whole.

### 7. Spot the Mistake

*(I make some mistakes and challenge you to identify them.)*

This can be difficult to understand. If this does not suit your learning style you could skip it.

Further Ideas: Some people do not deal with abstract ideas very well. For this or other reason(s) they might get confused by an exercise like this. Typical responses I have seen include students with poor hearing that do not hear me say it is wrong and then think they have been taught an alternative. Also, if a student is distracted by still reflecting on the learning from an earlier exercise (which I approve of as they are then trying to take responsibility for their own learning) then they might misunderstand. I would avoid using a "spot the mistake" type exercises if I sensed that it was not working well for a particular class.

### 8. Stepping on Alternate Feet

*(We always step with one foot and then the other.)*

This has been talked about a lot already but it is so important it gets a little section of its own! Waltz has an 3 beats to a bar and you have 2 legs; So you end up starting each bar with a different foot.

## Section D: Dance Naturally

No Dance Naturally section is included in this lesson as there was plenty of repetition during the skills section.

# Waltz Beginners Solo Practice (Extra Exercises for Leader) (Ballroom)

There is a YouTube video https://youtu.be/m0RhMiue0YA that fits with this lesson plan. The numbered sections of the video and this lesson plan match to make working with both easier. For most students I recommend watching the video and regularly pausing (and maybe rewinding) as you also read this lesson plan. However, depending on your learning style, you might develop a better approach for you. Note, the video is designed so you can join in using a smaller space such as your living room.

## Section A: Introduction

### 1. Introduction

*(Extra ideas for the leader.)*

This short video covers two issues just for the leader for individual practice for waltz. Really it is very brief and there is not much content. However, I wanted to have these two reminders of the feet position as I think it is so important.

## Section B: Warm Up

Obviously you can do your own warm up. Although this is a short lesson anyway without any practical exercises to copy.

## Section C: Skills

### 2. Feet Position With Partner

*(A demonstration of how the foot position looks with a partner.)*

A demonstration of how the leader's feet go each side of the follower's right foot when dancing offset to avoid collisions between the knees and feet.

Further Ideas: There can be confusion between the position left-to-right and the position forwards-and-backwards. The feet are close when looked at from behind but if looked at from the side they may still be far apart.

### 3. Waltz With a Broom

*(A broom makes an excellent dance partner that will not object to being trodden on during practice.)*

In the quickstep leader's solo practice video I demonstrate how to practice with a broom as a follower. You could do a similar thing to practice waltz, in particular the skill of tucking around the follower's right foot.

Further Ideas: The broom does not exactly copy the behaviour of the follower's right foot because it does not move away when the leader steps with the left. However, I find it is a good learning tool.

## Section D: Dance Naturally

Obviously you can do you own practice of the feet position over and over to make it feel natural.

# Waltz Improvers 360 Turn to the Right (Ballroom)

There is a YouTube video https://youtu.be/EjMTvU3POyA that fits with this lesson plan. The numbered sections of the video and this lesson plan match to make working with both easier. For most students I recommend watching the video and regularly pausing (and maybe rewinding) as you also read this lesson plan. However, depending on your learning style, you might develop a better approach for you. Note, the video is designed so you can join in using a smaller space such as your living room.

## Section A: Introduction

### 1. Demonstration

*(The move is introduced and demonstrated.)*

It is possible to turn to the right and keep dancing waltz. We will learn to do it in 6 steps, keeping the same timing as for the things we have already learnt.

Further Ideas: A demonstration helps many students. Depending on learning style it may be almost impossible to process or understand something until the whole thing has been demonstrated.

### 2. Beware of Getting Dizzy!

*(We are learning to turn in only one direction so be careful.)*

You might just practise this for a few minutes every time you do some dancing. Then over a few weeks it will come together. Many people say that they get less dizzy generally once they have been learning to dance for a while.

Further Ideas: I find some people just do not realise getting dizzy is a bad thing. So, just to be sure I explain this before a lesson like this. In particular, in the learning progression this might be the first lesson where this is an issue. However, as a teacher I might forget things like this so I try to have a robust way of warning students (which also helps protect me from being sued). In the case of the videos notice I always refer viewers to the description for health and safety advice.

## Section B: Warm Up

### 3. Warm up Dance

*(Get the basic waltz running nicely before trying to add a new thing.)*

During this lesson the leader's right forward step will be where the move is initiated. So, during your warm up perhaps try saying "right" every time that happens.

## Section C: Skills

### 4. Leader Steps Without Music

*(We go through the steps individually and then without stopping.)*

Although I like to use "watch and copy" as much as possible in my teaching this is something where I am aware that many people prefer to see it broken down.

Further Ideas: In a group or private class I will watch the students carefully and pace how fast I go through this material to fit their learning speed.

### 5. It Will Feel Different With a Partner

*(Don't practice that too much yet!)*

As soon as we can we will start dancing this in couples so that your body can start learning how to step around your partner and also out of the way of your partner where necessary.

Further Ideas: I think it is generally a good approach to do as much practice as possible of the basics. This is a rare case where I want the leaders to "barely have the hang of it" and then start dancing with a partner. There is a lot to learn including when to give space for the partner to move into and when to themselves move around the follower. I find too much solo practice makes these much bigger problems as they will have got too used to not having a partner.

### 6. Followers Can Choose not to Learn Their Steps

*(You might try to just step where you are led.)*

This lesson is designed around the follower learning their steps as well. This is partly because it is a learning technique that I think is better suited to a a self-learning resource. However, if you are the follower you might try the alternative of not learning your steps and allowing yourself to be led by the leader.

Further Ideas: I think that in the long-term it is better to get the followers just following. If I have a teaching assistant I might get them to go and work with the followers on lead-follow exercises while I teach the leaders their steps. Or I might take the lead-follow exercises while someone else teaches the steps. It would depend on who I had available to help probably.

### 7. Follower Steps Without Music

*(Dance the steps individually and then to a rhythm.)*

Leaders probably do not want to join in with this or it can get confusing.

Further Ideas: Really, I do not let leaders join in except in exceptional circumstances. I just find it makes things far too confusing.

### 8. Opposite Foot, Opposite Direction

*(A quick reminder of what the leader was doing.)*

The follower began the move by stepping back with the left foot. So, the leader must have stepped forwards with the right foot.

Further Ideas: I am partly doing this to help any leaders who are getting too distracted by the follower's steps. Reminding students of something that was covered a few minutes ago is often useful but beware of "and remember the shape for leaders is this" turning into 30 seconds of talking which can then just confuse students more (who want to just get on with it).

### 9. Follower Go Back With Left After Turn

*(Yes you go back with the left after the turn.)*

Followers (and leaders) you dance alternating from one foot to the next. This remains true even if you just finished a move.

Further Ideas: I find this is worth mentioning again and again. I particularly find that if a student has learnt with another teacher that did not deal with timing then the student may have the "assumption learnt from outside the class" that during moves the basics of the dance (such as timing) no longer apply.

### 10. Follower Steps Stamping

*(The follower steps are stamped out to make each step clear.)*

I demonstrate clearly where each step is. This can also help leaders as you should also be taking a step every time the follower takes a step.

Further Ideas: I always try to remember to emphasise that stamping is "just a learning tool and not how we actually dance".

### 11. Dance Together

*(How the leader and follower dance together.)*

I particularly look at how the leader and follower must sometimes take large and sometimes take small steps. This is either to get around your partner or give your partner time to get around you.

## 12. Why 360 Turns?

*(I discuss this controversial topic.)*

You may choose to start doing turns that are less than 360 degrees. Definitely do that if it works for you. My experience is that students appreciate the simplicity of initially learning a full turn and then may just turn a bit less once it starts making sense. Most people do not do full 360 turns when dancing waltz.

Further Ideas: I teach this with a full 360 turn mainly because I found that when it was not 360 degrees students would often get confused about which way to face afterwards. Being able to give the simple instruction "face the same way after the turn" is great. I also find it helps that the leader and follower simply swap places twice during the move which is also easier to understand for a beginner than talking about positions on a clock or points in the room. After a bit of practice I then make it clear that turning less is fine and will try myself to model not getting all the way around so they can see it is ok.

Further Ideas: A typical way to teach this is in combination with turning to the left as a move that is a series of 4 sections where you end up facing the same way you started. I am not keen on this for many reasons. (1) I find it takes up a lot of room on the dance floor and seems to often get in the way of other dancers. These other dancers will often get out of the way meaning the couple doing the move never realise they are creating such havoc and getting in people's ways. (2) I prefer to break down the learning into smaller chunks so that the student has more freedom to combine them in different ways. (3) I still remember when I learnt this for the first time and for the stage I was at it was too much to remember (the steps, the leads and the facing at each point of the move). It became a really big deal for me (and other students) and I think we were distracted by it for far too long and that this was a barrier to other fun stuff in waltz and I believe it was a moment when quite a few people gave up the classes.

## 13. Leader Steps Without Music (Repeat)

*(We go through the steps individually and then without stopping.)*

Extra practice.

Further Ideas: My experience with this move is that a repeat of the individual practice is helpful.

## 14. Follower Steps Without Music (Repeat)

*(Dance the steps individually and then to a rhythm.)*

Extra practice.

Further Ideas: I find the repeating of the follower steps is less important (as in theory they are being led and also I find the follower is already learning to adapt and fit around the leader meaning they don't have to know the steps so well). However, I have repeated them for this lesson partly because of the limitation of a self-teaching video lesson of me not being able to see my students.

## 15. Stepping More And Less During the Turn

*(Another look at when the leader and follower take small and large steps.)*

This is a key thing to make the move work better.

Further Ideas: I find this is a key place where a teacher can see from a distance and help even the fastest learners perform better. This is similar to the input I give to students learning the cross body move in latin.

## 16. Underturning

*(Most people I see dance less than 360 degrees.)*

It is fine to do less than 360 degrees. We only did 360 degrees initially to make it easier to learn.

Further Ideas: I already covered the "360 degrees controversy" earlier. Yes I know some people think I am teaching it "wrong". I believe that I am not teaching any "bad habits". If a student ends up in a local community where this move is always danced with a different total rotation I believe they can very easily adapt.

### 17. Dancing Along a Line

*(We can think of this as dancing on a line with one person getting out of the way.)*

This same idea is seen in other dances such as the cross body move in latin.

Further Ideas: This is one of the fundamental reasons I think learning the 360 version is the best introduction to this variety of move. Yes a strong student can probably think in curves and angles already. But for the average student I think a line is quicker and easier to understand. Students and teachers can use the line as a foundation and change the angle later. If you are a teacher intending to change the angle (during a series of classes) I encourage you to do so as soon as possible to prevent the formation of habits that would be difficult to break. I always introduce different angles myself as soon as I can for this same reason (so that students are not stuck in one mode of doing the move).

### 18. Advanced Ideas

*(Optional thoughts for dancers who like to analyse.)*

You might have no idea what I am talking about in the video for part 18 of this lesson. However, I know some analytical students will find this quick discussion useful.

Further Ideas: This is something I often share with students who show an interest individually during the class rather than to the whole group.

### 19. You Could Only Do Half This Move

*(Something for later development.)*

Just so you know, it is possible to only do the first three steps of the 360 degree turn. This means only doing the first half of the move. Then you the leader could dance backwards around the dance floor. You could also do slightly less than 180 degrees and end up at an angle and do something else instead. I absolutely do not recommend this yet (if this is your first attempt at this lesson). The exciting potential of partner dancing is that as you get weeks, months or years of dancing experience you can keep learning new things by continually chopping up moves, changing moves and improvising: And for me personally, I enjoy my dancing much more now that I dance almost completely improvised all the time.

Further Ideas: (1) I sometimes like to briefly mention things that will happen later in a student's learning. I find many students benefit from this. A side-effect I do not like is that some students get very keen to learn the advanced thing straight away. My general experience is that those most keen to jump ahead to advanced things are some of those least able to do so and this means I almost always have to say no. (2) I would rarely mention this if a class was finding the move difficult because I am then trying to make everything as simple as possible (and I do not want to intimidate them with the idea what they are doing has to get more complicated because it absolutely does not because the advanced choices are only choices and not necessary).

## Section D: Dance Naturally

You are welcome to find a song to practice to.

# Waltz Improvers 360 Turn to the Left (Ballroom)

There is a YouTube video https://youtu.be/EnRSzUoEpKI that fits with this lesson plan. The numbered sections of the video and this lesson plan match to make working with both easier. For most students I recommend watching the video and regularly pausing (and maybe rewinding) as you also read this lesson plan. However, depending on your learning style, you might develop a better approach for you. Note, the video is designed so you can join in using a smaller space such as your living room.

## Section A: Introduction

### 1. Watch and Teach Yourself

*(Watch this after the "360 Turn to the Right" video.)*

If you have worked on your turns to the right here are a few bits of learning to help you do the same thing but instead turn to the left.

Further Ideas: The main reason this lesson is so short is that the corresponding video had to be cut short for technical reasons. However, it turns out this is fine because I have adapted this to an alternative teaching technique I often use for situations where we are learning a "variation of something we have already learnt". If you are a teacher you might choose instead to use an adapted version of the "360 turn to the right" lesson plan.

## Section B: Warm Up

Obviously you can do a warm up dance or similar. Perhaps practising the turn to the right would be useful.

## Section C: Skills

### 2. Watch, Copy, Watch, Copy, Watch, Copy

*(Watch and copy and bear in mind three important things.)*

For this lesson I challenge you to watch and copy. If you are confident with the 360 turn to the right you can now perhaps teach yourself the 360 turn to the left. Three key things to look for are: (1) Notice it begins at the start of a bar. To clarify, it begins "at the start of a set of three steps". (2) The leader starts the move on the left foot (which must be at the start of a bar). (3) The leader turns to their left.

Further Ideas: (1) I genuinely think this is an ideal opportunity to use the "watch and copy" teaching approach. If you are a teacher, remember you can go around and give individual help where necessary (although I encourage you to be patient and let your students work through the problems). (2) When you go to give individual help you might try to give "extra information" or a "learning tip" rather than simply walk them through what they should do. Giving "help with learning" and not "help with this particular move" can help nurture the "watch and copy" skill which is part of what they are learning in this lesson. (3) With my class I will usually explain that "this might take slightly longer but how cool will it be for you to have also learn the skill of watching and copying" because "how amazing will it be to be able to watch other dancers and copy what they do".

### 3. Underturning

*(Most people I see dance less than 360 degrees.)*

It is fine to do less than 360 degrees. We only did that initially to make it easier to learn.

Further Ideas: I am mentioning this in the lesson to prevent an early habit forming of "always doing exactly 360 degrees".

### 4. Stepping More And Less During the Turn

*(A look at when the leader and follower take small and large steps.)*

This is a key thing to make the move work better.

Further Ideas: I think this is a key thing a teacher can help with even for fast-learning students.

## Section D: Dance Naturally

You could obviously choose a song to practice to.

# Waltz Improvers 360 Turn Both Ways (Ballroom)

There is a YouTube video https://youtu.be/X56vCKtazLI that fits with this lesson plan. The numbered sections of the video and this lesson plan match to make working with both easier. For most students I recommend watching the video and regularly pausing (and maybe rewinding) as you also read this lesson plan. However, depending on your learning style, you might develop a better approach for you. Note, the video is designed so you can join in using a smaller space such as your living room.

## Section A: Introduction

### 1. Leader Introduction

*(Learning to turn both ways means learning which foot you are on.)*

Whether you turn to the right or left depends on whether you are stepping with the right or left foot on the first beat of the bar. You then need to instantly "feel" or "remember" which of the two similar moves to do. This is not easy!

Further Ideas: This can be very difficult and for some dancers it may be effectively impossible due to the combination of skills involved. In particular I think this is something students need to be "ready for" meaning maybe the class has done the turns for a few lessons (perhaps 10 minute sections of ten lessons in a row, meaning maybe three months for a typical weekly class) before trying this. I would expect to be able to push private students faster as I could tailor the learning to them better.

### 2. Follower Introduction

*(You just need to follow.)*

Followers, this lesson is not really for you. But hopefully you can dance with the leader as they try to learn the skill.

Further Ideas: (1) I have had the occasional attempted "mutiny" from bored followers (often women) during exercises (or whole lessons) like this. The trouble is that I think they were mutinying against a fundamental feature of partner dancing that has evolved over hundreds of years. And it seems to me this mutiny is going to be difficult to achieve! Even when I dance with a very experienced follower and manage to share "leading duties" spontaneously in the dance it can still go horribly wrong sometimes. It just seems to be a thing that whenever partner dancing evolves there is either a set sequence for the whole dance or one person has to lead. We are learning the version where someone leads (which I find to be more creative, musical, interpretative and fun) and that inevitably means the leader has to be the focus of some of the lessons. (2) Sometimes this mutiny defends itself by claiming the leading is sexist because the man leads. Well, notice I never say "man" but say "leader". I regularly have women learn to lead in my classes specifically because it means they can enjoy the dancing more (because it is more challenging and because they can be more expressive and have more control over the choices in the dance). The final argument I then often hear is "but I want to dance like in the books/movies" or "but I want to dance with a man" in which case, well, a logical analysis of this shows they are the ones bringing the "sexist ideas" to the dance floor and I don't really think I can help them beyond keep trying to convince them to try leading (and often I get a lady who already dances leader to spend some time talking to them).

## Section B: Warm Up

You could warm up by revising the two turns. Or, if you think your learning style better suits it (I think mine would), you could just do a couple of warm up dances and come to the turns fresh.

## Section C: Skills

### 3. Demonstration Dance

*(I demonstrate the two turns.)*

As I do the demonstration I talk through what I am thinking. I try to share what the key things are that I think, feel and do to make the moves work better.

Further Ideas: Many students find a demonstration dance where I talk through what I am doing very useful. This is a technique I mainly use when teaching more technical things. I think the problem with doing this with beginners is that many do not have the skill of "watching and copying".

### 4. Leader Individual Practice

*(Join me as I keep stopping at the start of different bars of music and work out which way to turn.)*

As you get more practice of this you might either decide it is too complicated and does not suit your way of dancing or some people find it starts to feel natural and they don't have to think about it any more. Remember that if it does not suit you, it is fine and there are an incredible number of other things to learn in partner dance.

## Section D: Dance Naturally

You could obviously dance to a song and practice this skill.

# Waltz Improvers All Forwards (Ballroom)

There is a YouTube video https://youtu.be/SiBi5q0oji0 that fits with this lesson plan. The numbered sections of the video and this lesson plan match to make working with both easier. For most students I recommend watching the video and regularly pausing (and maybe rewinding) as you also read this lesson plan. However, depending on your learning style, you might develop a better approach for you. Note, the video is designed so you can join in using a smaller space such as your living room.

## Section A: Introduction

### 1. Extended Introduction

*(The move is introduced and demonstrated.)*

Taking only forward steps is fairly easy to understand. Hence this is a short video and I cover a lot in the introduction.

Further Ideas: (1) I really think there is not much for the teacher to do here beyond introduce the idea and (strongly if necessary) remind students to beware of colliding with other couples on the dance floor. I have on rare occasions taken a couple off the dance floor and worked with them on safety before letting them back on again. (2) Did it seem like I was vague about whether to join in or not in the video? That was on purpose. I simply left it so that students would do whatever suited them better (obviously some might want clearer instructions but in that case I imagine they would not join in because I did not say to do so and I think that is probably the best choice in general for most students).

## Section B: Warm Up

You could obviously do your own warm up first.

## Section C: Skills

### 2. Join in or Watch

*(We demonstrate a few times.)*

Manage your own learning by watching or joining in with each demonstration.

Further Ideas: I am using the "join in or watch" technique here on purpose because I think "all forwards" is a relatively simple thing to learn compared to the level of student who will likely be watching the video.

### 3. Demonstration Dance

*(A brief demonstration of how you might use the move.)*

We dance basic and sometimes take all forward steps.

Further Ideas: If this had not been a simplified demonstration I might have used the check after the forwards steps to go into something dynamic such as a turn. As you break from going forwards you are decelerating and if you allow that deceleration to continue it can flow nicely into another move, especially if you allow a curve to develop during the deceleration.

Further Ideas: By "allow that deceleration to continue" I mean that if something decelerates to zero and continues changing it will then start accelerating in the opposite direction, like bouncing off a wall. I like to create this sense of a "bounce" to make my dancing have smoother shapes. There is a technical physics/engineering term called "jerk" which is the "rate of change of acceleration" and that is what I am actually talking about here. By allowing a "bounce" to occur there is less jerk and so the dance is smoother.

### 4. Watch Out Ahead!
*(Careful please!)*

Some final thoughts: (1) I only personally use this if the dance floor is fairly empty and there is a big space. (2) If the dance floor is crowded I usually prefer to use one of the rare spaces that open up for something else instead. (3) Another couple may have seen the space and also be doing a fast move into it so still watch for danger.

Further Ideas: If one of my students crashes into someone I feel just as bad as if I did it. I think I banged feet quite a lot as a beginner until I self-taught to take smaller steps.

Further Ideas: I try very hard not to collide with other dancers. However, it still occurs sometimes. (1) The biggest problem I have is with followers who are "out of hold" and step backwards without me leading it (this is something I have never fully been able to prevent and even pulling back if I am still holding with one hand can simply make some followers twist the backwards movement). (2) In a rare one-off my partner once fell to the floor when they went into a "drop move" that I had not led and fell away from me (which I now watch out for and find I have time to prevent). (3) Finally, I have 10 or 12 times in the last ten years myself had me or my partner make contact with another dancer from another couple for various reasons. (a) Sometimes I put an inexperienced follower into a turn during which I cannot lead their position (as they are trapped into a set pattern) and this can mean they are "out of control". If this happens I will generally not lead them into such a move again. Sometimes during the move they are so "out of control" a collision occurs. (b) Sometimes I change my dancing after a follower has complained about my dance style (perhaps it is too boring for them) when this style has actually been dictated by the traffic on the dance floor. And then a collision occurs because I am not respecting the "spirit of the dance floor". (c) Very rarely I find it is impossible to avoid a collision if two or three other couples are dancing badly around me and my space disappears. In this case I often bring my partner close, stop us from dancing (which if a follower is inexperienced or not very willing to follow unusual moves can be difficult), try to turn my back towards the impending collision and brace for impact!

## Section D: Dance Naturally

You might choose a song to practice this to.

# Waltz Improvers Curved Basic (Ballroom)

There is a YouTube video https://youtu.be/Rsn8KfnCrTY that fits with this lesson plan. The numbered sections of the video and this lesson plan match to make working with both easier. For most students I recommend watching the video and regularly pausing (and maybe rewinding) as you also read this lesson plan. However, depending on your learning style, you might develop a better approach for you. Note, the video is designed so you can join in using a smaller space such as your living room.

I would typically teach this after at least 6 months of learning waltz. So, although I have called it an "improver lesson" I think it is for covering after dancing for a while.

## Section A: Introduction

### A Fundamental Skill in Partner Dancing

*(I use this a lot in my social dancing.)*

I have included this as an improver lesson because I find that beginners will do this movement too large and this can place strain on the knees of the follower and also simply look odd. Also, when I briefly tried this the need to curve a particular direction (when already thinking about the feet a lot in waltz) seemed too difficult for many students.

Further Ideas: I consider key benefits of curving the basic in waltz to include: (1) Forming "blocked leads". (2) Adding shape to otherwise straight steps. (3) Giving the shoulders something to do which I think is fun. (4) Building a disconnect between the legs and shoulders that then helps with dancing skills in general. Finally, note that I do it almost all the time but usually the movement is so small you can barely see it even if you are looking for it.

### 1. Shoulder Movement is Difficult and Not Everyone Does it

*(This is optional.)*

Firstly, I have observed that many teachers find this difficult to teach and I am finding it particularly difficult with a self-learning resource so please bear with me! Secondly, some people like this and some people don't. You might make your choice about whether to do it based on your personal preference or you might decide based on what people local to you do so that you can fit with the social scene better.

Further Ideas: This is perhaps the thing I most often accidentally teach wrong. So, if you are a teacher you might want to watch out as well! However, I am a big fan of this. It relates strongly to the concept of "block leads" which I like a lot as I find that if done well they are a very gentle way of leading and also because they only "block certain directions/movements" I find they give the follower a certain freedom to make their own choice of one of the "non-blocked" directions/movements.

### 2. This is Quite Bitty

*(This video is about a difficult topic.)*

This topic is unusual and I have not managed to make the video as streamlined as the others. My main tip to help is that there are approximately two phases to the lesson: (1) A focus on shoulder and foot skills. (2) How to apply those skills to the first step of the bar in waltz.

Further Ideas: I would usually choose either a feet or shoulder emphasis for the lesson based on the students. In the case of this self-learning lesson I have "hedged my bets" (as I cannot tailor it to you) and done both to help make it useful to both styles of learning.

### 3. Exaggerating

*(In this video we exaggerate the movements.)*

A subtle shoulder movement looks to me (and to many others I have met) much better than a large shoulder movement. Also, I think a large shoulder movement then starts to dominate the dancing too much when it should be a small element compared to other things. I aim for the shoulder movement to be very difficult to see to a casual observer. However, I suggest learning the movements at first by doing them large and then making them smaller as you get better.

Still not convinced? Think about learning to write. Children learn to write with large letters and only over time does their writing get smaller and neater. I think you can draw analogies with learning almost any physical skill. So, learn this curve larger and then later on make it small and neat.

Further Ideas: My experience is that this is controversial! Some people seem very upset that I teach an exaggerated version first. However, I have confidence in my approach because it seems to mirror so many other physical skills that are learnt with simplified, larger movements first and then simplified later.

### 4. The Direction of Curve is Important

*(Many people do this wrong.)*

This is a video lesson so I cannot watch and guide you. Many people curve (and/or move their shoulders) in the wrong direction until I correct them. So, please take extra care with this particular lesson!

Further Ideas: Curving the wrong way is a very common mistake. My best guess is that (instinctively or based on thinking about it) students think it doesn't really matter which way they curve and so do not focus on this element. It may also be because it is difficult to see which way the curve goes.

### 5. Focus During Some Scenes

*(The camera was set up wrong during some of the recording.)*

Just so you know, some clips are slightly out of focus.

## Section B: Warm Up

You might dance one or more waltzes to music as a warm up.

## Section C: Skills

### 6. Quick Demonstration

*(A quick demonstration to show what we are aiming for.)*

The leader and follower are aiming to move together.

Further Ideas: This seems to me to be a good place to give a demonstration to avoid students spending ages learning the skills separately and possibly finding it difficult because they didn't realise something about how it fitted together.

### 7. Pushing the Opposite Shoulder Forwards as a Leader

*(As the leader walks forwards they can push the opposite shoulder forward.)*

When we eventually do this in the waltz we will only do this on the first beat of every bar and only if we choose to when going forwards. For practising we are doing it on every step as an exercise.

Further Ideas: This is a rare occasion where I am teaching with an exercise that is quite different to the final way it is used. This is mainly because I tend to teach this the same way in all situations (to make it easier to learn as a whole across a dancer's complete repertoire of dances) and in some other situations we do it on every step. Anyway, it seems easier to teach it on every step first because otherwise imagine being a beginner and trying to only do a new and strange movement once every three steps!

### 8. Pushing the Opposite Shoulder Backwards as a Follower

*(As the follower walks backwards they can push the opposite shoulder backwards.)*

Like the leader exercise but backwards instead of forwards.

Further Ideas: The leader does the same movement as the follower if moving backwards so in that way it doesn't do any harm to get everyone practising at the same time. But, if you are a teacher and you feel your students are likely to find this confusing (and in my experience most will be confused) then you could recommend that the leaders not join in and instead have a break.

### 9. Feet Position

*(Keep the feet position the same.)*

Because it is a curve the leader might be tempted to do something unusual with the feet. Avoid this temptation. Keep the feet the same as usual. Simply step as you were before.

Further Ideas: I often see leaders try to step "across" their partner or do something else. This is because the student is thinking that the difference in the shoulders might mean the feet are different as well. Again, this is not necessary and the feet should step the same as before.

### 10. Leader Steps Broken Down

*(We break down the leader steps individually.)*

The movement is broken down and looked at more slowly to suit some learning styles.

Further Ideas: I would not always do this and in "real life" classes I would decide based on the students.

### 11. Follower Steps Broken Down

*(We break down the follower steps individually.)*

Like the leader exercise.

Further Ideas: Again, I would not always do this but it depends on the students.

### 12. How to Use for First Step in Waltz

*(A demonstration with an explanation which you could join in with.)*

Watch this demonstration where I discuss the move. You could join in with this if you want. Alternatively you might pause the video to try it on your own.

Further Ideas: I am explaining this much more than I usually do other things when teaching dance. The reason is that my personal experience is people find this lesson more confusing than other lessons. So, I am using (1) visual demonstration and (2) spoken explanation with (3) the opportunity to copy. These three "choices for how the student can interact with the lesson" are intended to make this effective for many different learning styles.

### 13. But the Shoulder Thing is Different

*(Yes you could say it is.)*

I like to teach the shoulder movement at the same time as the curve because I think they are sufficiently related that it helps. But yes you could argue I didn't need to teach the shoulder skill at all.

Further Ideas: This is how I teach it. You might develop a different technique if you are a teacher. I'm not convinced I've yet found the best way. However, I am very convinced that the shoulder movement (the one that acts in the opposite way to the feet) is very useful in many areas of partner dancing (I know it really helps me with a lot of things in my leading) and that is why I "frame" this lesson around it. Perhaps it is coincidence (in terms of the underlying physics) that these two skills are sufficiently related to be taught together. However, I still think teaching them both at the same time is effective.

### 14. Leader and Follower Together

*(We break down the leader and follower steps at the same time.)*

A chance to dance the steps at the same time before dancing in hold. We break them down stopping regularly.

### 15. Leader and Follower Together (Continuous)

*(We dance the leader and follower steps at the same time.)*

Now we dance continuously without stopping.

Further Ideas: I usually find this is "carnage" and goes very wrong. However, I feel it is important to push on and let the students feel the "whole thing put together" as soon as possible even if we then have to go back and do more individual practice afterwards. I am always trying to avoid the mistake of "teaching it to perfection without a partner so that when my students have a partner in front of them they find something odd happens like they elbow their partner all the time because they got into the habit of an incorrect movement while there was no partner there to show it was wrong".

### 16. Practice Together to Music

*(Join in or watch with this practice dance.)*

A chance to do some continuous practice to music. Stop and start as you need to obviously.

Further Ideas: This is only a short section in this video (compared to the amount of discussion and demonstration time) but the viewers have the chance to pause and use music to practice so they can extend it.

### 17. Slow Walk Through as a Couple

*(A chance to join in or watch a slow demonstration.)*

This may or may not help your personal learning style. It is purposely at a different angle to some of the other partnered demonstrations.

Further Ideas: If I am teaching a group I am quite likely to use this exercise and get everyone to take each step together.

### 18. Only On Step One For This Application

*(A reminder that the curve is on step one.)*

It is different in different dances but in waltz the unique look comes from emphasising the first beat. So, the curve (that we are learning in this lesson) happens on the first beat to give an authentic waltz look.

Further Ideas: Remember this is a styling option I like to teach. In social dancing I find a bit of a curve is nice (and when you get more advanced it is a form of "trap lead" which I like). However, you may not want to dance waltz like this. Also, remember that after some practice the aim is to make this curve tiny (effectively impossible to see) and we are only learning it this large in the lesson to begin with.

Further Ideas: I emphasised this on its own for video purposes. In a real life class I can monitor this (and many other things) and give specific advice as necessary. I generally try to give bits of advice like this during exercises so my students are not standing around listening (so it feels like something we are chatting about briefly and not "an annoying thing the teacher is making us listen to for ages preventing us from dancing"). However, I would not generally shout out the advice during "practice dances" as they will be concentrating and in that case I usually try to succinctly say it in just one or two sentences after the practice dance is over and before the next part of the lesson.

### 19. How it Works Socially

*(This pattern is usually quite easy for followers to pick up if led well.)*

I find this is a fairly popular thing to add at social dances. I like to repeat it 3 or 4 times and then carry on for a few more repetitions to give the follower a chance to work out what is going on and then join in.

Further Ideas: Obviously this means making the movement larger. So, to clarify. I typically curve every first step a very tiny amount (invisibly small) all the time. And sometimes I do it slightly larger (but not too large) as a nice shape for a few bars.

### 20. Shoulder Movement can be Difficult in Waltz

*(This might not work for you.)*

This just does not work for some people and so if you are finding it difficult I suggest just giving up as there are plenty of other options.

Further Ideas: One of the key reasons I try to discourage those finding it difficult from persisting is that I think this works best if the curve is small. Learners finding something difficult will often compensate by making the movement large and so easier to do (which by the way I think is a great strategy which I encourage). However, in this case, if this is done with large curves (and perhaps also a little clumsily or out-of-time) then I think it can look not very good and is not fun to do.

### 21. Practice Time

*(Debbie and Andy show how it can look.)*

For many people curving is much more fun than just dancing in a straight line. Debbie and Andy are very capable students (who I think make this look easy despite) but in general something like this is possible for most improver students with practice.

Further Ideas: In my real life classes I will use others for demonstrations where possible so that my students see other styles of dancing. A very common thing I have to do is tell individual students (or even the whole class sometimes) that they do not need to make their feet point out all the time. My ankle joints are unusual and my feet cannot come together at the front without being painful so my demonstrations often have slightly unusual feet positions. As a rule-of-thumb I would say "copy the large shapes" and let the "small shapes take care of themselves".

### 22. We Are Still Dancing Waltz!

*(All the usual skills still apply.)*

In with the earlier waltz lessons we are still aiming to stay with our partner and (for example) keep the feet offset to avoid collisions.

### 23. Tucking Around the Follower's Right Foot

*(Some more in depth details relating to the curve on the leader's right side.)*

We look at one example of how we are still using our waltz skills: tucking around the follower's right foot. This particularly relates to not knocking the follower off balance and not treading on the follower's feet.

### 24. The Role of Shoulder Movement in Trapping the Follower

*(This technique can guide/trap the follower to stay in a line.)*

This is another application of shoulder movement. By giving a lead in both directions (one way with the shoulder and one way with the feet) it can help trap a follower into a line. I find this useful with beginners to make following easier. However, I think you need to be really practised at this as a leader or else it may just confuse them.

Further Ideas: I'm mentioning this so my students who have seen this other common application realise there is a link with this curved basic. I find the curved basic is particularly good with beginners to control their dancing more and "scaffold" them into doing better dancing.

Further Ideas: This is advanced but I will mention it here. If you step forwards on one side this almost inevitably causes some twisting which can be interpretted as a lead to the side. For example, stepping forwards with the right foot can cause a twist to the right and how does the follower know this is not a lead to turn to the right? Pushing the left shoulder forwards (only very slightly) counters this right side lead (which is also only very slight) and means it feels like a forwards lead. This is what I mean by a "trap lead" created with two opposite leads that cancel each other out.

### 25. Avoid Also Forcing a Side Step in Waltz

*(Discussion about side steps.)*

This similar to and sometimes taught at the same time as a side step on the second beat. (Just to clarify, this discussion is to relate what I am teaching to how other teachers teach so if you are not familiar with the alternative way this is taught I think this will make no sense to you.) I recommend not forcing the side step for reasons to do with maintaining good lead-follow. Well, yes if you watch some of the demonstrations during the lesson there is a side step. But, I'm not forcing it and I am generally only allowing the natural momentum to let it happen. I am not forcing it.

Further Ideas: Learning one new thing such as a curve on the first beat can still fit in with leading and following. I find that if two steps are taught at the same time such as a curve and a side step then it can quickly become a habit (to think of them as a joined pair and not two separate things) and limit students for a long time as they get trapped into this single variation. I think the side step should be learnt in isolation and not directly linked (perhaps via "muscle memory" or a student's misconception) with something else. Mainly for this reason I think that for best medium-term benefits it is better not to learn a side step at this point.

### 26. Shoulders Still

*(A useful skill is keeping the shoulders still.)*

It is up to personal taste but moving the shoulders all the time can get tiresome. Also, varying your styling (for example in this case varying the amount of shoulder movement) gives you more variety in your dancing.

Further Ideas: (1) The "shoulders still" idea is highlighted to emphasise that the shoulder movement is only an option (and should not look large). Sometimes I find a student tries too hard and makes large shoulder movements all the time. (2) One thing I would say though is that every time they learn a new thing it will likely look odd for a while. So, as a teacher you have to let them "look odd" for a bit before jumping in to help. I might wait at least half an hour (or even a few lessons) depending on circumstances. (3) Despite all the problems caused by shoulder movement, I still think it is right to teach it for the long-term benefit. However, in a typical "real life" class progression I would typically not cover this until they had been learning for at least 6 months.

### 27. Remember Only on Step One

*(A reminder that only step one is different.)*

This means steps two and three are simply danced as we learnt before.

Further Ideas: I am repeating this because I think it is a common mistake to try to curve all three. I think it also acts to re-emphasise other aspects of the movement.

### 28. Followers You Actually Wait to be Led

*(I've been waiting to say this.)*

So, now is time to say to the followers "you do not need to think about the shoulder movement". And it is only really a lead so you do not have to also do it anyway! (Although as with all leads you will typically have it influence your movement so you will likely end up doing it, but without really thinking.) So, basically you can forget about this lesson and only the leader needs to remember. However, because you practised the movement you should naturally do it a little bit in response to the leader. Doing this lesson will have made you a better dancer as your body is ready to respond to a "shoulder-isolated lead".

## Section D: Dance Naturally

### 29. Practice Dance

*(We dance and you could join us.)*

You might practice to a song with us.

Further Ideas: I find that this skill can take a long time to learn and often needs leaving and returning to days or weeks later. I find individual practice is often ineffective as students can often start turning the wrong way and I find myself running around unable to keep up with correcting the mistakes in everyone.

# Waltz Improvers Leader Backwards (Ballroom)

There is a YouTube video https://youtu.be/VlbKW5Q5Pa0 that fits with this lesson plan. The numbered sections of the video and this lesson plan match to make working with both easier. For most students I recommend watching the video and regularly pausing (and maybe rewinding) as you also read this lesson plan. However, depending on your learning style, you might develop a better approach for you. Note, the video is designed so you can join in using a smaller space such as your living room.

## Section A: Introduction

### 1. This is Unusual

*(This is not a typical thing that I have seen other teachers cover.)*

You may choose not to do this lesson. It covers an unusual situation that when it does happen is potentially very dangerous.

Further Ideas: I teach dancing backwards a lot to my students as I think it improves the potential for improvisation. I often see other dancers with fantastic opportunities offered by the dance floor that they cannot take advantage of because they would need to initially backup slightly. I consider this to be true in ballroom and latin.

### 2. Learn This For Those Rare Moments

*(You could learn this anyway to help you out occasionally.)*

In football/soccer many players train heavily in the techniques for scoring a goal. However, they may only score a goal once every 5 hours or more of play. This is a similar situation as the leader may not dance backwards very often but it is a great skill to add an occasional special shape/pattern to your dancing. I would estimate that I dance backwards about once every 2 dances and it almost always creates a special moment in the dance as I am able to continue a flowing movement and therefore maintain musicality.

Further Ideas: (1) Based on teachers I have watched, about half of them do teach the leader to dance backwards but usually this is only as part of a larger move and not done as a separate skill. (2) I think it is an important skill but I carefully manage my class and I try to predict "overenthusiastic" students who might be dangerous and either speak to them separately or purposely teach this on a day they were not in the class.

### 3. Foot Position is Important

*(I recommend having good foot position skills before doing this lesson.)*

The ability for the leader to have their feet tucked around the follower's right foot helps keep the feet tidy and safe. When the leader dances backwards the footwork can be more challenging, so I recommend only doing this lesson if you are feeling fairly confident with the position of your feet.

## Section B: Warm Up

### 4. Foot Position Recap and Extension

*(Revise the position of the leader's and follower's feet.)*

Leaders practice tucking their feet each side of the follower's right foot. We also practice this for the new situation of the leader travelling backwards.

Further Ideas: As I say elsewhere in my lesson plans, I have found this is a "succinct and effective" way to teach foot position. If I were doing a paper for a teaching journal I could go into much more detail but for students of social dancing I think a single, clear message is best.

## Section C: Skills

### 5. Build From On-the-Spot to Dancing Backwards

*(This is similar to how we learnt to travel forwards.)*

Start dancing on the spot then slowly introduce a backwards movement on the first step of every bar.

Further Ideas: I tried for a while teaching this during the first lesson thinking it would be easy to learn at the same time. It was easy to learn but there were complete beginners dancing backwards around the room which was not very safe. I now delay teaching this for many weeks or months. If I were doing a private lesson I might do it sooner, but only if the students clearly understood the forwards steps were the ones to use when social dancing.

### 6. Follower Shoulder Pull

*(Safety awareness for followers.)*

Followers, if you see danger you can pull on the shoulder of the leader to hold them back and say something like "collision" or "watch out". I often have partners do this when I am already aware of what is behind me and I'm about to do a check but I still appreciate the pull because it seems better to be safe than sorry.

Further Ideas: I find most followers realise to do this anyway but it seems worth mentioning.

### 7. Leaders Look Backwards

*(Look around!)*

My head is often moving when I partner dance socially. I have had my partner tell me this is "wrong" and that I should hold my head steady. However, I believe it is very correct for social dancing because it means I can stay aware of the dancers around me and avoid collisions. When I am dancing backwards I sometimes have my head turned all the time looking backwards which might not win a competition but I think it wins the appreciation of the other dancers as they know I am looking where I am going!

Further Ideas: Wow I'll try not to get too excitable about this. If you are teaching students to dance socially I recommend encouraging the leader to look around. Actually I rarely even have to do that because if I don't say anything about the head I find they do it anyway as it is a sensible way of staying safe. Oh, and while I'm at it I don't ask the followers to bend their back and look to the side for two reasons: (1) Many find it uncomfortable. (2) I think a great aspect of social partner dancing is chatting to your partner and it seems nice to look at each other while you do it (while obviously glancing around as well as necessary).

## Section D: Dance Naturally

### 8. Practice Song

*(A chance to practice as we dance in the video.)*

Do not try to copy exactly. The demonstration dance is to generally remind you what it should look like.

Further Ideas: As usual I give individual practice time of a new skill. I am using a practice dance for this self-learning lesson. With a group class learning to dance backwards I might instead line up the class to go down the room in a straight line together and also have the followers looking out for collisions.

# *Waltz Improvers Leader Curve Backwards (Ballroom)*

There is a YouTube video https://youtu.be/8PBsd1ldlnI that fits with this lesson plan. The numbered sections of the video and this lesson plan match to make working with both easier. For most students I recommend watching the video and regularly pausing (and maybe rewinding) as you also read this lesson plan. However, depending on your learning style, you might develop a better approach for you. Note, the video is designed so you can join in using a smaller space such as your living room.

## Section A: Introduction

### 1. Small Curves

*(I try to keep the curve small because I feel it reduces the chance of injury and makes it look better.)*

Stretching too far can stretch or damage muscles or tendons. I therefore recommend not curving too much. I am going to be demonstrating this in an exaggerated way to make it easier to see: So you do not have to curve as much as me.

Further Ideas: In a class I am often saying "I'm exaggerating this so you can copy more easily" as a continual reminder. It only needs to be a throwaway comment that is not too distracting and I would only ever say it while doing something else so that it is not an "annoying thing the students have to listen to instead of actually learning".

### When to Teach the Curve

Further Ideas: I would hope that I had introduced dancing backwards (the lesson that I do before this) at a time when the students were ready for it. I would then look to teach the curve as soon as possible afterwards so that the instinct to apply a slight curve was built from the very start. I find that if a curve is taught too late after introducing the same move without a curve it can be difficult (or for some impossible) to learn. However, there is a balance as I find the basic movement without the curve needs to be fairly good first. I suspect this is something that will vary from teacher to teacher as much may also depend on their overall teaching style.

## Section B: Warm Up

Maybe warm up by doing the "Leader Backwards" lesson or the "Curving the First Step" lesson.

## Section C: Skills

### 3. Optional Curve

*(Leaders you might try curving backwards .)*

If you have already done the curving lesson then you might try curving the backwards step. Be careful of how far round you stretch as it can be very awkward. This is definitely optional and I would generally only curve very slightly (almost invisibly) myself. And often when travelling backwards I do not curve at all because the backwards steps won't last long and there are other priorities in the dance.

Further Ideas: I would rarely teach this but have included it for completeness. It seems sensible to highlight that it can be also done backwards. I have definitely noticed that some students are bad at managing the amount of things they learn at once. Many of them will not get the sense that something is too difficult and keep trying. This is an example of something I am wary of introducing for that reason.

### 4. Optional Curve Direction Practice

*(Extra practice at knowing which way to curve.)*

Help with getting a feeling for which way to curve.

Further Ideas: This scene in the video is an attempt to recreate the kind of "question and answer" session I might have when teaching something like this. I would only be teaching it to relatively experienced dancers and I would tailor the "polishing exercises" to their specific needs.

## Section D: Dance Naturally

You might find a song to practice to.

# Waltz Advanced Using Rumba as Variation (Ballroom)

There is a YouTube video https://youtu.be/njT5m1P7SJU that fits with this lesson plan. The numbered sections of the video and this lesson plan match to make working with both easier. For most students I recommend watching the video and regularly pausing (and maybe rewinding) as you also read this lesson plan. However, depending on your learning style, you might develop a better approach for you. Note, the video is designed so you can join in using a smaller space such as your living room.

## Section A: Introduction

### 1. Waltz and Rumba Both Use Three Steps

*(Waltz and Rumba combine well.)*

Because they use the same number of steps we can use rumba moves to a waltz rhythm. It means we have to drop the pause but otherwise it should work.

Further Ideas: I find this can work well with a mixed-ability class.

### 2. Follower Turn Health and Safety Warning

*(The follower turn here is done in only three steps.)*

The turn I teach here is done in only three steps. Followers if this is not comfortable for you then please skip this lesson or maybe turn in six or nine steps with leaders then coming out on the appropriate foot. You should not force a turn if it is uncomfortable.

Further Ideas: I have a global reminder of only doing what is comfortable at the start so this is not necessarily essential from a legal point of view but I like to reinforce the message sometimes.

### 3. This is an Advanced Lesson

*(I teach fast.)*

I think this is potentially dangerous on a social dance floor as you are going to be moving unpredictably (compared to typical waltz) so I have made it an advanced lesson. I have therefore chosen to teach the content fairly fast.

Further Ideas: In a "real life" class I can tailor the lesson to the students. I often also like to start by demonstrating something and seeing if people can do it. If they can I've just saved time and my students haven't had to be patronised by me for a few minutes. This demonstration technique is not an opportunity to "show off" by demonstrating something difficult and then making the students feel like they are not very good. But I think it is an opportunity to show something they might realistically be able to get, help them develop their "watch and copy skills" and also boost their confidence.

## Section B: Warm Up

You might do a practice dance (or more than one) as a warm up.

## Section C: Skills

### 4. Putting New Yorkers into Waltz

*(Something easy to start with.)*

We break out of waltz to do two New Yorkers and then continue with waltz again.

Further Ideas: This is an example of where I am trusting my students to understand how learning works. I do not particularly like this move but I think it is a good one to start learning with. I would hope they then did not use it too much in social dancing.

### 5. New Yorker Combined With a Turn
*(Adding a turn.)*

A slow turn in waltz is something I often see in social waltz as a variation. Here is an example of how to include one. By using a New Yorker as well it gives it more energy compared to some other variations.

### 6. A More Complicated Example Routine
*(You can do whatever you like. Here is another example.)*

Generally I dislike using example routines. This feels like the kind of topic where they are useful. I have purposely chosen an example here which progresses around the room meaning something like this can be used even if you are in a situation where you need to keep progressing with the flow of the dance floor. You need to know cross body move for this. I start with two demonstrations (one straight through and one with me talking) to give you the initial big picture.

Further Ideas: Teaching a routine like this is typically something I only do with more experienced groups. I would then ideally spend the second half of the lesson looking at how to vary it and also take elements from the routine on their own.

### 7. Some Other Thoughts
*(I like to include rumba into my waltz.)*

Some more thoughts about how I like to incorporate rumba into my waltz.

Further Ideas: I have resisted the temptation to waffle on too much in this video. In a class I often do a demonstration of one or two minutes and then invite questions to make it more interactive and try to stop me from talking about things the class are not interested in.

## Section D: Dance Naturally

### 8. Free Practice Time
*(Do not copy us just practice on your own.)*

You can see us having some fun with rumba steps in waltz to this dance. Do not try to copy exactly what we are doing. Instead I recommend doing your own free practice with maybe us dancing just being useful to remind you of the timing or a few ideas as you dance.

Further Ideas: In my advanced classes I often do little demonstration dances so my students can watch and then ask questions based on what they saw such as "that thing you often do after the turns how does that work" or "how did you know the quiet bit of music was coming up" or "we haven't done the thing where the leader turns at the same time can you teach it". But for free practice I would come around helping and have only put a demonstration dance here for the video. The only exception I can think of is that I might repeat the routine once at the start of the free practice so students who want to can watch it again.

# A Course of Lessons in Latin Dancing

Latin dancing can mean many things. For this book it means rumba, salsa and cha cha. Depending on which country (or region) you dance in, latin might be mainly danced on-the-spot or as a larger shape. This book looks at dancing on-the-spot as a variation but mainly teaches a commonly-danced "larger" version of latin which I find is generally clearer and easier for beginners to copy and learn.

If I am teaching in a small space or I feel in the mood I will teach what I consider to be the more "shady nightclub or back street bar" version of just dancing on-the-spot in a very relaxed way. If this is how you want to dance I recommend still using my lessons and simply choosing to use the on-the-spot basic most of the time in your dancing. A more advanced approach I like is to do a very tiny back basic (stepping back maybe an inch) which I find stylistically much nicer than on-the-spot (as it gives a small amount of movement) and I also find means I can activate the rest of my body more easily as I dance.

There are many similarities between the 3 dances. I strongly encourage learning rumba first. Salsa is arguably then just rumba danced faster. Cha cha then adds two extra, faster steps at the end of each bar which is typically easier to learn after first becoming confident with the simpler footwork of the other 2 latin dances.

The 3 latin dances are covered separately in this book, however remember that a skill or move learnt in one can usually be used in the others as well. There are also additional lessons covering skills applicable to all latin dances:

Rumba

Salsa

Cha Cha

Latin Solo Practice

Latin Improvers Cross Body Move

Latin Improvers One or Two

# Learning Rumba (Latin)

With a slow rhythm, rumba is a good dance to start with. There is time to think. Also, if you step, for example, a tenth of a second too late it might not be a problem: but stepping this late can be confusing in something like salsa where you have less time between beats.

There are 5 lessons in this book covering rumba:
Rumba Complete Beginners
Rumba Beginners Forward-and-Back Basic
Rumba Beginners Slow Turns and Dance Arounds
Rumba Beginners Rotating Forward-and-Back Basic
Rumba Improvers Travelling Side Basic

# *Rumba Complete Beginners (Latin)*

There is a YouTube video https://youtu.be/QxCCL9tbslQ that fits with this lesson plan. The numbered sections of the video and this lesson plan match to make working with both easier. For most students I recommend watching the video and regularly pausing (and maybe rewinding) as you also read this lesson plan. However, depending on your learning style, you might develop a better approach for you. Note, the video is designed so you can join in using a smaller space such as your living room.

Further Ideas: There are two stepping drills that I sometimes use when teaching rumba. They are parts 6 and 9 of the salsa complete beginners lesson. I recommend these particular stepping drills if the student is struggling to either take clear steps, keep up with the music or get a feeling for the individual steps.

## Section A: Introduction

### 1. Rumba is Easy!

*(You will just be dancing together to a simple pattern.)*

We will do some exercises first to learn to hear the music and move in time. Then very quickly you will be dancing rumba like this.

Further Ideas: Many students like to see what they are aiming for so they can better manage their own learning. In a "real life" class I might not do a demonstration for the simple reason that the first exercise is already rumba. I'm doing it for clarity in this self-learning resource.

## Section B: Warm Up

### 2. Watch and Copy Back Basic

*(Let's just start straight away by watching and copying the basic step.)*

We will break this down later. First rewind the video a few times if you need to and keep trying to copy what I am doing. It will probably go wrong the first few times but keep trying!

Further Ideas: My experience teaching this type of dancing to beginners is that if I stop to explain something a majority of the students get frustrated. An effective approach for most learners seems to be to see it and keep trying to copy. For most early beginner lessons I mainly try to give students space to manage their own learning. The only problem here is if a student has poor self-learning skills and maybe just dances along knowing it is wrong but "hoping it will get better" which it probably won't without a good strategy. If enough of the class are not managing their own learning very well I will get more bossy and impose stops, starts and maybe (in rare cases) break down the individual steps. If only a few students are struggling I will often use individual help during "free practice" dances to support them.

## Section C: Skills

### 3. Back Basic Together

*(Dance back basic together.)*

Now we have got the steps sorted we can try dancing them together. It will be like looking into a mirror as your partner does the opposite steps.

Further Ideas: Yes I really have just dived straight in! My personal experience of teaching rumba/latin is that this is the best approach. If a student is struggling I resist the temptation to break it down and simply continue whilst repeating the mantra "stop and start again if anything feels weird". There are compelling arguments for breaking it down: However, all I know is that giving the students the whole latin basic immediately has worked very effectively for me as a teacher with the vast majority of the thousands of students I have taught.

### 4. Off and Back Onto the Paper

*(How the piece of paper helps.)*

You can think of rumba as repeatedly stepping off and then back onto the piece of paper.

Further Ideas: I have highlighted this verbally because it is a video. I would only mention this in a class if I thought it was needed: ideally the class will simply see it and copy. Something else I often say to classes at this point is "you do not have to copy me exactly, just the general idea" particularly if I sense people are making adjustments to their already correct stepping to try and mimic me more. And if keen students in the class ask for more I often say "variations, styling and other options can be covered later if you want" and maybe speak to them individually later because for me this first class is for the less-skilled students to get a first try in a simple learning environment.

### 5. How Many Steps?

*(How many steps are you taking?)*

Well, it depends on exactly what the question means. A lot of people think of rumba as being three steps. And they think of those three steps as being spread over four beats of the music.

Further Ideas: I like to have a discussion here. I think it is very important to let students think about it the way that works for them. If they are dancing correctly and they think of it as two steps then that is fine at this stage. I have seen students try to change how they think about it and then start going wrong: this can be a fantastic learning experience at a later stage but early on I just want to help them get dancing and have fun.

### 6. Step On-the-Spot Individually

*(Stepping on the spot is generally more difficult but a good exercise to help with learning.)*

Try stepping on the spot with me. You will need to time it with the music and step on the same side as me each time.

Further Ideas: I use this exercise here for a number of reasons: (1) It is a break from "partner work". For example, it gives me full control of the group and means I can push the agenda of good timing without any couples tempted to ignore it (which I think is totally fine but I like to guarantee some quality time on it early with a skilled dancer to copy from). (2) I find some students are confused by the combination of feet hitting the ground and moving during the back basic and that this on-the-spot exercise is often a breakthrough for them as they can isolate the "feet hitting the ground skill". If this is an issue I often mention something like "this feeling of stepping is the same for all of your rumba so remember the feeling and aim for it whilst doing, for example, back basic as well". (3) Again, without the distraction of the backwards and forwards motion I find some students have a breakthrough during the exercise in their understanding of the pause.

### 7. On-the-Spot Basic Together

*(Dance on-the-spot basic together.)*

This is great training in varying the length of your steps. It can also help to have to do the timing and other skills without the back step so that the skills start to become clearer and separate in your mind.

Further Ideas: I used to be tempted to skip this and I find the learning is fine without it. However, I really like the way this helps the slower learners (who are maybe not used to the idea of symmetrical dancing with a partner or even dancing at all) build up from the previous exercise with just the one additional element of being in front of your partner. Again, this can be a breakthrough as some students experience something like: "Oh so when I'm dancing with someone this is all we are doing; I get it now!"

### 8. The Shapes We Make

*(We look at some of the shapes made when dancing rumba.)*

Seeing how it looks at moments in the dance can help you to learn. For example, you can look for those shapes in your dancing.

Further Ideas: I like to use shapes as it is a form of visual learning that can be reinforced with words at the same time (and note that I am happy for students to ignore what I am saying if they want to focus on the visual learning).

### 9. Back Basic Together (Repeat)

*(Dance back basic together for a second time to get it really good.)*

If it is getting boring that is a good sign that you are getting good!

### 10. Changing Between Back Basic and On-the-Spot Basic

*(Another thing to think about! Try varying your basic step.)*

This is optional but I strongly recommend that you try it anyway. This will help you learn to take different-sized steps.

Further Ideas: This exercise evolved from me trying to teach my students to vary the length of their steps. It gives a new dancer an instant way of varying their dancing and so feeling less bored.

### 11. Different Hands When Dancing as a Couple

*(Some people find they can ignore this when starting to dance which I think is best. But you might find the issue distracts you in which case here is an explanation.)*

There are lots of different ways to hold hands while dancing rumba. For example, you could hold both hands, only hold hands on the closed side or not hold hands.

Further Ideas: I will generally only cover this in a group class if I can spot people getting distracted by it, or if they are trying to copy my hands exactly (which I do not encourage) or if the question is asked.

### 12. Do Not Overextend the Back Leg

*(Reaching with the back leg can feel nice but many styles of latin are softer than this.)*

Reaching a long way backwards as you step can make it easier to feel the timing. It can also be fun. But! At this stage the fun will come from dancing to a whole song in time with your partner. Reaching back a long way is a "short term bit of fun" that (in my experience) most agree gets boring after a while and most agree does not look very good.

I discourage a long backwards step for three main reasons: (1) It can make dancing to fast music difficult. (2) My personal preference is for a subtler form of latin which has smaller steps (and I like to share this with my students). (3) If you are on a crowded dance floor long back steps can cause you to keep kicking the people behind you.

Further Ideas: Some styles of latin do reach back more aggressively. However, given the health-and-safety issues and the problems of dancing to faster music I think smaller steps with less reach are better. Also, I have noticed that dancers who extend a long way back often do not do this to faster music so I would argue they are using a variety of options for different music and so I would argue that to keep things simple for a beginner it is best to teach them the one option that works for a variety of speeds of music (especially as a common complaint I hear from beginners that are taught by other teachers is that they cannot dance to fast music). I like to say "step back only 50% as far as you actually could", "be lazy", "could step further but I won't", and so on.

### 13. Standing Offset

*(I think this is advanced but that it can help some beginners.)*

Depending on how you are dancing this might help but I think most beginners can ignore it. Basically, if you stand slightly offset as you are facing each other it means you are less likely to tread on each other's feet or crash knees.

Further Ideas: This is an example of something I like to mention as a "throwaway comment with a bit of highlighting" so that the seed is placed in their mind for something that can crop up later as they learn more. I hope it means they are already a little bit prepared for this and so will be able to learn it more quickly when the time arrives. I mainly find this can be a problem with knee-banging for some beginners (but most seem to dance far enough apart that it is not a problem) and I find making them stand offset can make the "mirroring" more confusing and on balance I choose to make the mirroring easier and run the slight risk of knee-banging.

### 14. The Best Exercise I Have Found

*(Perhaps go back and repeat this exercise.)*

Changing between on-the-spot basic and back basic is the most useful exercise I have found for teaching rumba and all latin. If you want to do 5 minutes practice a day (a great approach to continuing your learning and getting to the point where you are confident and can enjoy your dancing) I generally recommend just doing this one exercise. Also, "stop and start again" whenever you need to which if you are just starting out might be every 20 seconds which is fine and better than continuing after you have lost the timing or stepping or something else.

Further Ideas: If I am warming up a beginners class who have already done one or more lessons I often do so with this exercise.

## Section D: Dance Naturally

### 15. Stop and Start Practice

*(We dance rumba and keep stopping and restarting.)*

Starting is a particular skill. You need it to actually begin dancing and also to cope with problems during the dance. Here we practice this skill. This exercise also builds awareness of the different parts of the dance.

Further Ideas: I think this helps a lot of students improve their timing because they keep having their attention drawn to it and also because this is sort of an advanced timing exercise. I find it does a lot of other good things too. For example, I think new dancers are going to regularly have to restart their dancing after stopping for some reason during a social dance. This exercise gives lots of practice at restarting.

### 16. Keep Dancing for a Whole Song

*(Time to enjoy our new skills to a whole song!)*

This is great consolidation and fun to do. Stop and start again if anything feels odd. Eventually you might find you can adjust things as you go without stopping.

Further Ideas: I try to give my students plenty of individual practice time like this. In the world of teaching theory I am not sure what current thinking is on the most effective techniques but I do know that in a situation where a student will have to work on their own most of the time without an instructor (such as with a hobby like partner dancing) it is important to allow the student to develop self-learning skills. Free practice with the option to call the teacher over is useful for developing this. Also, many of my students do not go social dancing and have told me they want free dancing time in the class even if it is not effective learning because they want to experience that part of the hobby. Keen learners who want more guidance can always call me over for help during free practice so they have a different experience.

### 17. Keep Dancing for a Whole Song (Repeat)

*(The same exercise as earlier.)*

Another chance to practice.

# Rumba Beginners Forward-and-Back Basic (Latin)

There is a YouTube video https://youtu.be/QoM7oFfv6Bk that fits with this lesson plan. The numbered sections of the video and this lesson plan match to make working with both easier. For most students I recommend watching the video and regularly pausing (and maybe rewinding) as you also read this lesson plan. However, depending on your learning style, you might develop a better approach for you. Note, the video is designed so you can join in using a smaller space such as your living room.

## Section A: Introduction

### 1. This is a "Basic Step"

*(You might simply dance this one move continually and have fun.)*

The "forward-and-back basic" is a "basic step". Other teachers might describe it differently. However, what is generally true is that it is like a canvas on which you put more advanced moves. Are you stuck? Do you want something simple to dance while you warm up? Do you want an easy option so you can chat to your partner? Just do a basic step, perhaps forward-and-back basic.

Further Ideas: I find this is easier to teach than back basic in that the leader and follower force each other to do the opposite (as the leader goes forwards the follower must go back or tension will develop in the frame of the dancing couple). I find this is harder to teach than back basic because a beginner cannot simply look down and "copy what they see in the mirror". So, overall is forward-and-back basic or back basic the best one to learn first? My personal experience is that back basic is the best one to learn first for the majority of students.

## Section B: Warm Up

### 2. Join in or Watch

*(The basic step is simply forwards on the left and backwards on the right.)*

Join in or watch to pick up the basic movement. Unlike in back basic you go forwards on one side and backwards on the other.

Further Ideas: Again, this is another place where I find a "join in or watch" exercise is very effective. Yes it can be really tempted to share wisdom, perhaps things that really helped you when you were starting out, but my experience is that about 90% of students, given about 2 minutes to keep trying, stopping, watching and restarting will get it. I then usually find most of the rest will get it if I keep doing a "stop and start again" exercise and the remainder I will help individually while the rest of the class are doing free practice with a partner to music.

## Section C: New Skills

### 3. Foot Position

*(Slightly offset feet help avoid collisions between the knees and feet.)*

Because you are stepping towards your partner as you go forwards it is good to have the feet slightly offset. I teach this as the leader having their feet either side of the follower's right foot. And the follower having their feet slightly apart.

Further Ideas: Is this really important? On balance I think it is. Some teachers might think I should explain it a different way but I find "the leader having their feet either side of the follower's right foot" is a simple message that is easily remembered. I usually find that while learning this the follower will actively offer their right foot and help the leader which I like as it means everyone is learning and remembering together.

### 4. Practice Together

*(Dance forward-and-back basic together with us.)*

This exercise gives you plenty of time to join in or watch as we dance forward-and-back basic. If it feels wrong, probably just stop and start again. A good place to join in is when the leader is about to step forward on the left.

Further Ideas: I will often use this exercise with a group and allow people to do their own thing instead if it suits their learning style. I might then stop demonstrating halfway through the dance if people were doing well and start going around to help individually.

### 5. Shape of the Forward-and-Back Basic

*(How the leader and follower step together.)*

A lot of people think of this basic step as the leader and follower always stepping in the same direction. It is not a mirror in the same way as back basic.

Further Ideas: For a group or private class this might not need mentioning. For a self-learning resource I have added it just in case.

### 6. More Practice Together

*(Dance more forward-and-back basic.)*

Another chance to keep practising this basic step.

Further Ideas: It can be difficult knowing how much practice people need or want. I often ask my class directly and let them tell me!

### 7. Stop and Start Exercise

*(Dance forward-and-back and keep stopping and starting again.)*

This is both a good challenge and also extra practice of how to start which is a lot of people find useful.

Further Ideas: I like to use this to support students that are finding the timing difficult. It can also retrain students who are not stopping enough when something starts to go wrong

## Section D: Dance Naturally

### 8. Changing Every Four

*(Four back basics and four forward-and-back basics repeated for a song.)*

Get really comfortable with the forward-and-back basic by dancing it for a whole song mixing it with back basic.

Further Ideas: (1) If you have just learnt a new move repeating it for a song like this can really consolidate it and give the confidence to use it in social dancing. (2) Long term I encourage you to improvise and change what you are doing based on the dance floor, the music and other reasons. For an exercise and for practice when you are starting out a repeated pattern can be very helpful.

### 9. Changing on the Left

*(Changing between back basic and forward-and-back basic on the leader's left.)*

If you get used to changing on the leader's left it can help you change in a more improvisational way. Rather than just counting it out you can instead respond to the music and find the right moment.

Further Ideas: I am aware that "changing on the left" in many ways contradicts my passion for teaching my students to "improvise". So, why am I introducing this rule that has the downside that it is another thing to remember? The reason is that I find it fixes so many things. If you analyse the different moves they are all very similar when the leader is stepping on the left, so if the follower does not pick up the change it is unlikely to result in a collision. Also, many other teachers (and myself) teach certain moves, such as the "cross body move" starting on the leader's left foot so I feel it is good to introduce a "highlighting" of this point in the dance early on in preparation. Finally, I have experimented with not teaching this way and have simply found that "changing on the left" seems to be very effective in my experience! Also, I find my more advanced students eventually self-teach to change in other places in the dance as well and I anyway later introduce the idea that it was only a "learning tool for beginners" and not a rule to keep to forever.

**10. A Practice Dance**

*(Dance whatever you like to this song.)*

A song to dance to. You will see us dancing in the video but that is just to give you a visual reminder and optionally you might copy.

Further Ideas: I think it is important to give lots of free practice time, especially at the end of a lesson. In a "real life" class I generally go around giving individual help to people who still need support (and also to give further input to fast learners who want more).

# Rumba Beginners Slow Turns and Dance Arounds (Latin)

There is a YouTube video https://youtu.be/2VN83reYkDw that fits with this lesson plan. The numbered sections of the video and this lesson plan match to make working with both easier. For most students I recommend watching the video and regularly pausing (and maybe rewinding) as you also read this lesson plan. However, depending on your learning style, you might develop a better approach for you. Note, the video is designed so you can join in using a smaller space such as your living room.

## Section A: Introduction

### 1. Introduction
*(Beware of being dizzy, use a loose hold and these are slow moves.)*

Try to vary the direction you turn to avoid getting dizzy. This means leaders need to be careful how strongly they lead. Use a loose hold in case you get a bit tied up. Finally, these are intended to be slow moves and the footwork is not advanced enough to be able to turn fast.

Further Ideas: This is a way to introduce some fun moves for beginners. It only works if they hold back and do them gently. To turn and stay in time and stay safe while turning fast you need advanced footwork techniques.

### 2. Beware of Stepping Backwards
*(Careful leaders!)*

If your partner is dancing behind you do not step backwards or you might step on them! In this case you will be dancing "on-the-spot" instead of "forward-and-back".

Further Ideas: This might seem obvious but a learner can be concentrating on many things and could easily not realise they are in danger of crashing into the person behind them. This is anyway covered later by the structure of the lesson where immediately the idea of doing "dance around" with a partner is introduced, the person not moving dances on-the-spot.

## Section B: Warm Up

### 3. Forward-and-Back Basic Warm Up
*(Dance forward and back basic to get your bodies warmed up.)*

I like forward-and-back basic as the basis for these moves. I think that if you try to combine them with back basic they can feel a bit odd. But maybe you will find you can make them work.

Further Ideas: As usual, I start the class with a warm up. My personal teaching rule is to launch into this very quickly and resist the temptation to stand talking to my students. I always think they come to dance not listen to me!

### 4. Change Between Forward-and-Back Basic and Back Basic
*(Practice changing and maintaining timing.)*

We will be changing between different moves in this lesson. This is practice of changing and staying in time with the music.

Further Ideas: This is also a good excuse to practise a useful skill for beginners!

## Section C: Skills

### 5. Learn Dancing Turns

*(Turn on the spot while keeping the same timing.)*

This move can be difficult if you have only learnt the back basic. However, this lesson assumes you know the forward-and-back basic so you will be used to stepping in different directions.

Further Ideas: If I teach this move earlier, perhaps to students who only know back basic, I often emphasise the need to dance on the spot while turning.

### 6. Learn Dance Arounds

*(Dance around your partner while keeping the same timing.)*

Take your time and dance around your partner. As you finish the move, take your time and relax and keep the steady stepping going.

Further Ideas: This is often one of the first more advanced moves that someone learns. In this case I repeatedly emphasise the need to take your time, relax and keep the same timing before, during and after the move.

### 7. Turns and Dance Arounds Together

*(Dance together and as one person does a move the other dances on the spot.)*

Learn to keep dancing and gently change from dancing on the spot to doing one of these moves. Then gently finish and rejoin your partner. If you can keep the footwork going the same all the time this is much easier.

Further Ideas: If you are a teacher and forgot to tell the students earlier in the lesson to dance on the spot they might step on their partner as they dance around.

### 8. Look at Your Partner as You Dance Around

*(In the dance around you are dancing in a circle so try to look where you are going.)*

The dance around can be awkward if you allow yourself to be distracted. Maintain your focus on your partner.

Further Ideas: This was a breakthrough when I found this simple way of explaining this move. It seems to fix so many things in a very simple way.

### 9. Keep Pausing

*(During the moves the timing stays the same.)*

I demonstrate what might go wrong if you lose the timing.

Further Ideas: Some students do not have a strong sense of the timing. In this case extended practice may be necessary or simply accept they will go out of time during the moves.

### 10. An Example Dance

*(Debbie and I do a demonstration dance and talk you through it.)*

Some ideas about how I use these moves in my dancing.

Further Ideas: (1) This can be extended into many additional lessons of ideas and example moves to teach your students. I prefer to mainly teach other things and let this be a little fun extra topic for students to play with on their own. I have a few favourite variations but generally prefer things like the cross body move and spot turn. (2) The main exception is that I will generally spend more time teaching things like this if running "party type" classes that are more fun based.

### 11. What to do After the Turn

*(This is technical.)*

When you finish a turn or a dance around I recommend being patient and keeping with the music. Instead of "oh I've finished let's do the next thing" I recommend "on the spot relax, on the spot relax" until you feel a moment to start doing a basic step again.

Further Ideas: Some people don't seem to get this. My feeling from watching them is that they are often not able to relax (for whatever reason) and simply "have to do the next thing" rather than dance on the spot and wait for the right moment. I work to create a relaxed atmosphere in my lessons but some people will still feel anxiety when learning or may have some kind of worry that people are watching (even though in a crowded room why would anyone be watching them). I tend not to try to help with this too much and if a student can't do it I have learnt to "let it go" as it is one of those rare dancing problems which I find is difficult to fix: and anyway I don't think it matters and is easily fixed later (especially if some emphasis has been placed on it so at least they know what they are aiming for). Let beginners have fun I say!

### 12. Three is a Magic Number

*(This is technical.)*

If you are an experienced dancer watching this then you should find that if you do a turn or dance around in 3, 6, 9 or any other multiple of 3 steps you will find you can smoothly go into the next thing. If you are a beginner don't worry about this yet! You might notice that Debbie is often dancing like this in the demonstrations for this video.

Further Ideas: This is a teaching point which develops (over the course of many lessons if I am teaching a group for a few weeks or months) into a key aspect of my teaching which is stringing together moves in any order you like but still sticking to the correct footwork.

## Section D: Dance Naturally

This does not have a dance naturally section. I recommend you find a song to practice to.

# Rumba Beginners Rotating Forward-and-Back Basic (Latin)

There is a YouTube video https://youtu.be/JRttfvG23rw that fits with this lesson plan. The numbered sections of the video and this lesson plan match to make working with both easier. For most students I recommend watching the video and regularly pausing (and maybe rewinding) as you also read this lesson plan. However, depending on your learning style, you might develop a better approach for you. Note, the video is designed so you can join in using a smaller space such as your living room.

## Section A: Introduction

### 1. Introduction

*(Some of you might do this slightly already. Beware of getting dizzy.)*

Some styles of rumba are quite strict and do not allow this kind of move. I personally like to dance like this to add more variety. Beware of getting dizzy if you turn too much one way without taking a break. Beware of injuring yourself if you turn too far in one step and if you are stepping with the leg that feels easier your partner will be symmetrically opposite and on the step which is more difficult to rotate with: So do not force your partner.

Further Ideas: I find the idea that when your stepping is easier your partner's might be more difficult during a turn is a common one. However, for beginners who are wrapped up in their own learning it can be easy to forget. So, I might do regular reminders of this health and safety issue during a "real life" class.

### 2. This Follows on From Another Lesson

*(This lesson does not recap individual skills.)*

We are not recapping forward-and-back basic danced individually. If that feels important to you I recommend going back to an earlier lesson and doing this one another time.

Further Ideas: If a group is finding dancing forward-and-back difficult I will pretty much never introduce the rotation. The reason is that I find many people find the rotation difficult. Only in a few rare cases have I seen people cope with this so easily that they could continue with the same level of confidence as when they were not rotating.

## Section B: Warm Up

### 3. Forward-and-Back Basic Warm Up

*(Dance forward and back basic to get your bodies warmed up.)*

Before learning to rotate it warm up by dancing forward-and-back basic on a line.

## Section C: New Skills

### 4. Learn to Angle the Basic

*(I think a slow rotation is generally best.)*

The leader steps forward with the left and turns slightly to the right. Simply continue this direction of rotation from then on for as long as you like. Beware of getting dizzy.

Further Ideas: This is the opposite of many of the turns you do in close hold for example in ballroom. I have never completely managed to intuitively understand why. For some reason when rotating in hold on the spot it seems easier to turn clockwise.

### 5. Which Way to Turn

*(Extra explanation.)*

Extra help feeling which way to rotate.

Further Ideas: Remember that if you are the teacher you probably have (1) much more experience dancing than your students and (2) probably you have some kind of natural ability in dancing that helped you decide to become a teacher. And it might seem obvious to you but I have met many dancers who can't feel which direction to turn. I am always patient and give them the time they need. In some cases they might not get the hang of it in which case I would usually suggest trying again the following week (if it was a weekly class). Also, this is why I like to cover at least 7 or 8 things in a single class as then a student is not expected to get the hang of all of them.

### 6. Don't Turn Perfectly

*(The turn will drift slightly if done properly.)*

Do not try to turn perfectly on the spot as this does not work.

Further Ideas: I often see people trying to do this. Obviously if they really want to then they should go for it. But I want to be clear with my students that you do not have to.

### 7. I Like to Rotate Most of the Time

*(In social dancing I am rotating most of the time.)*

If I am teaching I stay static most of the time to make copying me easier. If I am social dancing I rotate most of the time as I find it makes it more enjoyable and also because as the leader I find it helps me spot opportunities for more expansive moves as gaps open and close on the dance floor around me. However, this rotation is often very slow (maybe taking 20 or more sets of 3 steps to do a full turn).

Further Ideas: Some teachers are really not keen on this rotation. And you may also meet dancers socially who do not like it. And maybe you will decide you do not like it either.

### 8. Fast is Not Best

*(This is not a competition to go as fast as you can!)*

I do not generally recommend turning too fast or it can get boring and make you dizzy. My rotation is often very slow, perhaps one full turn every minute of dancing.

Further Ideas: I have learnt to mention this or many students seem to try and go faster and faster.

## Section D: Dance Naturally

This does not have a dance naturally section. I recommend you find a song to practice to.

# *Rumba Improvers Travelling Side Basic (Latin)*

There is a YouTube video https://youtu.be/xT8oBn2h8UI that fits with this lesson plan. The numbered sections of the video and this lesson plan match to make working with both easier. For most students I recommend watching the video and regularly pausing (and maybe rewinding) as you also read this lesson plan. However, depending on your learning style, you might develop a better approach for you. Note, the video is designed so you can join in using a smaller space such as your living room.

## Section A: Introduction

### 1. Why I Teach This in Rumba

*(Why I am teaching this in rumba.)*

Travelling side basic uses quite a bit of space and movement. This means that for many people it works best in a slower dance such as rumba. Dancing this in cha cha can be awkward because you have the quick steps to do already which already cuts down the time for something like a travelling side step.

Further Ideas: More athletic students will often have the core strength to do travelling side basic in all the latin dances.

## Section B: Warm Up

### 2. Warm Up Timing and Other Steps

*(A warm up where we recap the timing and some other steps.)*

The timing is very important for the travelling side basic. This basic step has a very different shape and so for many students (including myself) in a situation like this it is necessary to be extra careful of the timing as the new shape is learnt.

Further Ideas: The timing is often combined with the learning of the steps meaning the two can be done together but not separately. Therefore a new type of step can often mean needing to relearn the timing. I find that once I have learnt a certain number of different shapes my brain seems to understand that the timing is always the same and it can suddenly be easier.

## Section C: Skills

### 3. Watch and Copy

*(Try learning this by watching and copying.)*

Keep replaying this as many times as you need to. This is not the same as side basic. It is a different basic step.

Further Ideas: This is a fairly fast teaching style compared to other basic step videos. This reflects that I generally teach this later than other basic steps. The main reason I teach this later is because it does not follow the "off back onto the paper" pattern.

### 4. Side Basic and Travelling Side Basic

*(The difference between these two basic steps.)*

A discussion of the differences between these two similar moves. The side basic does not travel! The travelling side basic does travel!

Further Ideas: Some students will confuse this with the similar basic step, side basic. My experience is that when this happens talking about it rarely helps and it is better to drill each one separately in turn and it gives the student time to understand that they are very different. I find talking about the differences is confusing for most people. Obviously this is a generalisation.

### 5. Hip Movement

*(Hip movement during travelling side basic.)*

Adding hip movement can make the move more fun. This is often popular with followers.

Further Ideas: I have heard some very strong views on this. One reason people develop the idea that their way is correct is due to the history and culture of dancing. If there is a strong and distinctive style of salsa danced in one region of the world then someone dancing there may believe that to maintain the integrity of the dance you should dance that way and not change it. This is an interesting debate. The role of ticket2dance is to create a quick and effective introduction to lots of different partner dances. Other people are working to preserve specific cultural or historical styles of dancing and that is great too.

### 6. Example of a Fun Variation

*(This is a move you can really play around with.)*

Travelling side basic is often done out of hold. Being out of hold can give more space for creating different variations.

Further Ideas: I probably play around with everything in partner dancing to have fun when I am social dancing. However, this is one of the easier places to play around.

## Section D: Dance Naturally

### 7. Continuous Practice

*(Dance it over and over to really get it feeling easy.)*

Dance it continually with me while I talk through some aspects of the move.

Further Ideas: I like to talk during repetitive exercises like this. I tell my students that it is ok to ignore me. Optionally some students can listen if the things I am saying are helpful for them.

### 8. Stop Start Practice

*(Stop and start with me to really finish off the learning of this basic step.)*

Stop start exercises help you get used to what you are doing at different points in the move.

Further Ideas: I would usually only do this exercise if I saw people regularly going out of time in a class.

# Learning Salsa (Latin)

Salsa is like rumba but faster. For this reason I strongly recommend learning rumba first and each salsa lesson assumes you have already done the similarly-named rumba version. After doing these 2 lessons most students find they can also start copying other skills from rumba to use within salsa simply by dancing the same things to the faster rhythm.

There are 2 lessons in this book covering salsa:
Salsa Complete Beginners
Salsa Beginners Forward-and-Back Basic

# Salsa Complete Beginners (Latin)

There is a YouTube video https://youtu.be/ki4MLXAMmFE that fits with this lesson plan. The numbered sections of the video and this lesson plan match to make working with both easier. For most students I recommend watching the video and regularly pausing (and maybe rewinding) as you also read this lesson plan. However, depending on your learning style, you might develop a better approach for you. Note, the video is designed so you can join in using a smaller space such as your living room.

Further Ideas: I am not sure this should actually be called a "complete beginners" lesson! I don't think I have ever taught a typical group of students this from scratch in their first lesson mainly because the music is so fast. I have sometimes had groups who for some reason are good physical learners who can do this lesson immediately (with the extra content such as "how many steps" and "stop start practice" from the rumba complete beginners lesson) but it is not typical in my experience.

Further Ideas: My primary focus when teaching beginner salsa is to get the students dancing to fast music. This is where the "rapid weight change" exercises and other parts of this lesson originate from. Other teachers seem to teach more moves or other things. So, why do I focus on fast music? I am obsessed by helping students get dancing as fast as possible so they can enjoy social dancing: I think this keeps them in the hobby, means they can start doing meaningful practice much sooner and ultimately become better dancers. And when I have seen beginners at salsa social dances they always seem to be sitting out a lot of songs because "it is too fast".

## Section A: Introduction

### 1. Do the Rumba First

*(This lesson assumes you have already done the rumba complete beginner lesson.)*

I prefer to teach salsa by first teaching rumba and then saying: "Let's speed up the music and wow we are dancing salsa!" I think it really is that simple. This means many things are not repeated from the rumba lesson. Basically, learn the rumba lesson thoroughly and then do this salsa lesson!

Further Ideas: If I am teaching a salsa class I won't tell people they are learning rumba (or I find people can get annoyed). But after, say, 10 minutes I'll speed up the music and admit that actually this is salsa and as a bonus the dance they learnt first was rumba.

### 2. Is it Really That Simple?

*(Wait, is salsa really just faster rumba?)*

Well, you could say salsa is a bit different. Technical arguments can be made for why they are different. For beginners I think the main difference is that you need to take smaller steps because the music is faster so you have less time.

Further Ideas: Yes there are technical reasons why rumba speeded up is not salsa. But, when I watch social dancers I rarely see these technical differences. So, I like to be practical and simply get my students dancing.

## Section B: Warm Up

### 3. Rumba Recap

*(We recap the rumba basic step.)*

This is simply the exact same exercise we did during the rumba lesson.

## Section C: New Skills

### 4. Stamping the Basic Step

*(Some people find it helpful to see the basic step exaggerated like this.)*

Stamping means you can hear each step which can be a breakthrough for some students. Also, the steps can look clearer and this can be a breakthrough moment as some people suddenly see more clearly the sequence of movements that are happening.

Further Ideas: This is one of the most useful things I have found teaching latin. I try to do it for about 30 seconds and this often helps students that are finding the basics difficult. I often do this with more advanced moves as well to make the subtle steps (such as the fast on-the-spot steps than many advanced moves include) more visible.

### 5. Join in or Watch Together

*(We dance together for you to just watch or copy.)*

I think best way for you to learn this is for me to show you rather than talk for ages! You can join in or watch or do a bit of both depending on your learning style.

Further Ideas: It can be so tempting to try to explain things in words. My experience as a teacher is that you cannot know what is happening in the student's mind. I find describing a move very ineffective compared to just demonstrating it in time with the music.

Further Ideas: I would typically give my students another song or two after this exercise to practice in pairs on their own with me coming round to help. I have not included this in the video because people can rewind the video (or pause it and find some music to play) to achieve nearly the same experience.

### 6. Making the Backwards Steps Feel Easier

*(A simple exercise to get used to the backwards movement.)*

The backwards step has a particular feel to it. It is not typically a complete movement back transferring all your weight. Many people dance it as more of a rocking motion.

Further Ideas: I find this useful and often drop this exercise in many times during a class to keep loosening people up and getting them used to the feel of the dance. It is particularly useful in salsa compared to rumba because salsa is danced to faster music.

### 7. Small Steps Against Wall

*(Force yourself to take smaller steps.)*

Standing next to the wall gives you very little space. It forces you to take small steps.

Further Ideas: I find this very useful. It avoids using words and helps to get everyone understanding the idea quickly. It depends on the local dancing culture but smaller steps is typical in many latin dance clubs where it means you can dance to faster music and also not tread on other people's feet.

### 8. Your Body Knows Which Foot is Next

*(If you finish a step clearly the next one should sort itself out.)*

If you take one step with the left then if you transfer the weight you must next step with the right (and vica versa).

Further Ideas: I find this is worth mentioning as many students have not worked this out themselves. Even if it is not useful I find it can be good to talk about the feet in detail sometimes to promote thinking about the dancing. However, I would not spend too long on this in a "real life" class as I think it can take away from more important practice time.

### 9. Fast Step Training

*(Salsa can be fast and there are ways to make this easier.)*

If you are dancing to faster music you do not necessarily want to complete every step. You are changing feet but you are not moving your whole body.

Further Ideas: An alternative way to think of this is that (1) the steps are smaller and (2) the upper body is not moving. There is a concept in dance teaching called "body awareness": A good example is that if you ask a group of students to move their right shoulder, beginners might also move their ribcage, arm, hand and even head while an advanced student may be able to completely isolate their shoulder and not move anything else. So, if you are a teacher please be nice to beginners who cannot take smaller steps and/or cannot hold their upper body still: If their "body awareness" is not good enough then they cannot isolate the part of the body you are talking about and I find they often think they are doing what you are asking but simply cannot feel or see that they are not.

### 10. Try Dancing to Fast Music

*(Just for fun let's try some really fast music.)*

If you are finding this difficult but want to keep trying to make this work you could keep repeating the "Fast Step Training" exercise (number 9) and then trying this exercise again.

Further Ideas: I have put this in as a brief exercise but it can be an entire lesson on its own to prepare the students for realistically fast music that can be heard at some salsa clubs.

### Stop and Start Exercise Missing

*(As usual I am a big fan of this exercise.)*

Further Ideas: Mainly this is missing from the video because for technical reasons the footage I recorded could not be used. However, because it is also in the rumba lesson I do not think it is a serious omission for this dance resource. If you are a teacher I would recommend doing the stop start exercise for a typical salsa complete beginners class.

## Section D: Dance Naturally

### 11. Continuous Practice

*(We repeat the continuous practice exercise.)*

As usual, you can join in or watch. You might try stopping and starting again (with the starting again being joining back in with me).

Further Ideas: As usual, I am finishing with some practice time. In a group class I'd likely offer a free dance for practice and then go around helping.

# *Salsa Beginners Forward-and-Back Basic (Latin)*

There is a YouTube video https://youtu.be/JoRi1ECFKr8 that fits with this lesson plan. The numbered sections of the video and this lesson plan match to make working with both easier. For most students I recommend watching the video and regularly pausing (and maybe rewinding) as you also read this lesson plan. However, depending on your learning style, you might develop a better approach for you. Note, the video is designed so you can join in using a smaller space such as your living room.

## Section A: Introduction

### 1. Building on Rumba

*(This lesson builds on the same lesson for rumba.)*

In my group and private classes, I generally teach the forward-and-back basic in rumba first and then teach it in salsa. I say "teach it in salsa" but basically we just do the same thing but slightly faster. For some people this is awkward because the music is faster and for others it is easy. However, most people will find there is a certain speed where it gets too difficult!

Further Ideas: This is something that is a dedicated lesson in this self-learning resource. However, if I was teaching a "real life" class this would be just one component of a larger lesson plan.

## Section B: Warm Up

### 2. Join In or Watch Individual Practice

*(A demonstration to copy or watch.)*

I dance forward-and-back basic with a group and you can join in or watch.

### Section C: New Skills

### 3. Join In or Watch Together

*(A demonstration to copy or watch.)*

I dance forward-and-back basic with a group and you can join in or watch.

### 4. Dancing Together

*(Try dancing together with us.)*

Stop and start again if you need to as you join in or watch as we dance forward-and-back basic.

### 5. Breaking the Steps Down

*(A look at the steps danced together.)*

We look at how the individual steps look at each point in the forward-and-back basic. I stand on a piece of paper to help illustrate the direction of each step.

Further Ideas: I strongly recommend that teachers use a piece of paper for this type of demonstration. Forward-and-back basic can also be danced with a stretched third step so that it drifts off the piece of paper. As a teacher I like to stick with the piece of paper version so that beginners of all different abilities have the best chance to pick up the basic step. It is typically not until later that I show students the option of stretching the forward-and-back basic.

### 6. Stop and Start Practice

*(Try stopping and starting with me.)*

A quick stop and start exercise to test your understanding of the steps.

Further Ideas: I find this a great way to appeal to different learning styles. If I want to challenge a group I will stop and start more often and maybe also mix in other basic steps or moves.

### 7. Dancing Together (Repeat to Faster Music)

*(Another chance to practice this basic step.)*

I have designed this lesson for the average learner so you might want to repeat earlier exercises or find other music to get more practice if this learning speed is too fast.

### 8. Changing on the Left

*(We look at how to change between the different basic steps on the left.)*

I find a great technique (as discussed elsewhere) is to change on the left. I recommend this for beginners and improvers and eventually suggest advanced students (after maybe years of dancing) start also changing in other places.

## Section D: Dance Naturally

### 9. Continuous Practice

*(Keep dancing the forward-and-back basic to get it really comfortable.)*

A chance to really consolidate this basic step.

Further Ideas: I find a majority of beginners like an extended chance to work on their own dancing like this. They may simply dance, try their own stop and start exercise or do something else.

### 10. Regular Pattern of Forward-and-Back and Back Basic

*(Four of each over and over again.)*

Students who do this usually either find it helps give them something definite to do for a whole song while they are still learning or it just helps sharpen up their changes.

Further Ideas: I like this because it means students who find spoken instructions difficult or who find it difficult to keep seeing changes can settle into the pattern. Learning aims for this exercise include simply getting more comfortable and confident with the stepping. As mentioned elsewhere, this is a "learning pattern" and I recommend aiming to be more improvisational in your dancing as you get better.

# Learning Cha Cha (Latin)

Cha cha feels to me like it is between rumba and salsa in speed. And to make it more challenging there are an extra two steps danced quickly at the end of each bar! As a beginner I found it difficult to dance the extra steps and still feel like I was dancing (and not doing aerobics). Now I am used to it and (mainly by keeping my head level to make the weight changes easier) I find it a much easier dance.

There are 5 lessons in this book covering cha cha:
Cha Cha Complete Beginners
Cha Cha Beginners Forward-and-Back Basic
Cha Cha Beginners Side Basic
Cha Cha Beginners New Yorkers
Cha Cha Beginners Criss Cross Basic

# Cha Cha Complete Beginners (Latin)

There is a YouTube video https://youtu.be/1vE1TESspZI that fits with this lesson plan. The numbered sections of the video and this lesson plan match to make working with both easier. For most students I recommend watching the video and regularly pausing (and maybe rewinding) as you also read this lesson plan. However, depending on your learning style, you might develop a better approach for you. Note, the video is designed so you can join in using a smaller space such as your living room.

## Section A: Introduction

### 1. One of the More Difficult Latin Dances

*(I think this is best learnt after rumba.)*

I very strongly recommend starting with rumba. Cha cha is then like rumba but with two extra, faster steps added.

Further Ideas: A progression I like is to teach rumba, then salsa, then cha cha. I throw in the salsa second so that students easily see that the different latin dances share similarities. Then the cha cha third because I find that for most students it is the most difficult of the three.

## Section B: Warm Up

### 2. On-the-Spot Basic (Join in or Watch)

*(We start by dancing on the spot.)*

We learn the basics of cha cha using the on-the-spot basic.

Further Ideas: I like to start with on-the-spot basic as some students find that without the backwards step it is easier to see and understand the rest of the skills such as stepping and timing.

### 3. Watch and Copy Back Basic

*(Let's just start straight away by watching and copying the basic step.)*

We will break this down later. First rewind the video a few times if you need to and keep trying to copy what I am doing. It will probably go wrong the first few times but keep trying!

Further Ideas: My experience teaching is that if I stop to explain something a majority of the students get frustrated. The effective approach for most learners seems to be to see it and keep trying to copy. I give space for students to manage their own learning. The only problem here is if a student has poor self-learning skills and maybe just dances along knowing it is wrong and "hoping it will get better" which it probably won't. However I find most students know to keep trying different things and stopping and starting until they get it right. If enough of the class are not managing their own learning very well I will get more bossy and impose stops, starts and consideration of the individual steps but I think that on average this is not best for most people.

## Section C: New Skills

### 4. Back Basic and On-the-Spot Basic

*(Join in with changing between these two basic steps.)*

If you can change between these two basic steps it means you are learning to keep the rhythm and vary what you are doing. This is great progress.

Further Ideas: I like this exercise as I also find that it helps students who are still finding the timing of cha cha difficult.

### 5. Back Basic Side-by-Side

*(Join in with dancing the back basic steps side-by-side.)*

We dance the leader and follower steps at the same time. This is was designed for the video to help you see how the leader and follower steps work at the same time.

Further Ideas: I am doing this side-by-side in the video. In a "real life" class in a room I might just arrange everyone on each side of the room or possibly skip this completely.

### 6. Back Basic Together

*(Dance back basic together.)*

Now we have got the steps sorted we can try dancing it together. It will be like looking into a mirror as your partner does the opposite steps.

Further Ideas: I find that for many students, dancing with a partner suddenly makes things easier. So, if some are struggling to dance the basic step individually I will almost always push on to getting people to dance in couples. (This is different to the approach of many other teachers I have observed but strongly recommend it as I have found it to be very effective.)

### 7. The Shape of the First Step

*(You and your partner will step in opposite directions on the first beat of the bar.)*

If you are finding the back basic difficult this can be a great way to think about it. If you can get the first step correct the rest often just flows. Often the best thing to do if this is difficult is to return to rumba and get it working better before progressing onto cha cha.

Further Ideas: I find this a really useful way of helping beginners.

### 8. The Cha Cha is on the Piece of Paper

*(Help with understanding where each step goes.)*

The cha cha has two extra steps that makes it different from the rumba. They both occur on the piece of paper.

Further Ideas: I find this is a common question and/or issue for students learning the cha cha for the first time.

### 9. Cha Cha Practice

*(Dance to the music while I talk it through.)*

This is a great chance to join in and/or watch. You can stop and start as much as you need to. If you need to join back in I recommend waiting for the leader to be about to step with the left and joining in then.

Further Ideas: Dancing as a whole class can be effective. I am a fan of giving time for individual practice. However I also like this exercise which I also use as a chance to talk about things I wanted to explain (but by doing it during an exercise it does not force the class to stand listening but have something active to do at the same time). I always allow students with different learning needs to use the music for individual practice and not join in with the group if they need. Also, students who really want to listen to what I am saying might stop dancing for a while.

### 10. Cha Cha Practice (Repeat)

*(Repeat of the same exercise.)*

I find that this is very useful so I have repeated it.

Further Ideas: In general I repeat things if it looks like it will benefit the class. In the case of cha cha I find many people appreciate extra general practice time. In a "real life" class I would not normally lead the exercise at this point but put on music for people to practice to. I have tried to simulate this "practice time" experience in this self-learning resource.

## Section D: Dance Naturally

### 11. Stop and Start Practice

*(Dance cha cha and keep stopping and restarting.)*

Starting is a particular skill. You need it to actually begin dancing and also to cope with problems during the dance. Here we practice this skill. This exercise also builds awareness of the different parts of the dance.

Further Ideas: This can be very useful if you are a teacher with a class who often go off the beat or tend to start well but then lose structure.

### 12. Keep Dancing for a Whole Song

*(Time to enjoy our new skills to a whole song!)*

This is great consolidation and fun to do. You might be getting good enough to talk through with your partner while you are dancing and recover from mistakes without stopping. Or, you might still want to stop and start again which I strongly recommend as the best approach if you are in any doubt.

Further Ideas: Many of my students do not go social dancing and have told me they want free dancing time in the class even if it is not effective learning because they want to experience that part of the hobby. Keen learners can always call me over for help and learning input.

# Cha Cha Beginners Forward-and-Back Basic (Latin)

There is a YouTube video https://youtu.be/GCeSL20Npn8 that fits with this lesson plan. The numbered sections of the video and this lesson plan match to make working with both easier. For most students I recommend watching the video and regularly pausing (and maybe rewinding) as you also read this lesson plan. However, depending on your learning style, you might develop a better approach for you. Note, the video is designed so you can join in using a smaller space such as your living room.

Further Ideas: The stop-start, "regular pattern of 4" and "changing on the left" exercises could be used to extend a lesson about forward-and-back basic. Partly to avoid repetition with the rumba lessons (which you are encouraged to do before learning cha cha) these are not included in this lesson plan.

## Section A: Introduction

### 1. Start With Rumba

*(I recommend learning rumba first.)*

I recommend doing the forward-and-back basic lesson for rumba first. Then the salsa forward-and-back basic lesson. Then this one.

Further Ideas: The technical reason for this order is as follows. The rumba version introduces the student to the step danced slower so they have time for thinking and feeling it as they learn. Then the salsa forward-and-back basic lesson will help speed up the dancing. Then when the student dances the cha cha version the music will feel slower (as they are used to the faster salsa music) and find it less daunting to add in the two more steps needed for cha cha.

## Section B: Warm Up

### 2. Watch and Copy Forward-and-Back Basic

*(Join in or just watch this demonstration of forward-and-back basic.)*

I recommend replaying this as many times as you need to. Get a feeling for what the move is and try joining in. Keep stopping and starting as much as you need to.

Further Ideas: If someone has got past the complete beginners lesson my focus is on helping them with the newer things they encounter in the new lessons. For forward-and-back basic I see two key new things: (1) Sometimes we step forwards and (2) you also have to learn to keep alternating between forwards and backwards to a regular pattern.

## Section C: New Skills

### 3. Back Basic Side-by-Side

*(Join in with dancing the back basic steps side-by-side.)*

In preparation for learning forward-and-back basic we recap the leader and follower back basic steps.

Further Ideas: I am mainly including this so the viewer can get used to how the demonstration works. I find many students will get confused if a slightly abstract setup (such as standing offset like this) is introduced at the same time as a new move.

### 4. Forward-and-Back Basic Side-by-Side

*(Join in with dancing the forward-and-back basic steps side-by-side.)*

We dance the leader and follower steps at the same time. As the leader steps forwards the follower steps backwards. As the leader steps backwards the follower steps forwards.

Further Ideas: I am doing this side-by-side in the video. In a class in a room I might just arrange everyone on each side of the room or possibly skip this completely.

## 5. Forward-and-Back Basic Together

*(Dance forward-and-back basic together.)*

Now we have got the steps sorted hopefully we can dance it together without stepping on each other's feet too much!

Further Ideas: In a "real life" class I might get to this exercise sooner as I can go around helping individually and/or do more "real time" management of the learning.

## Section D: Dance Naturally

### 6. Free Practice

*(If you want more practice here is another song.)*

An opportunity for free practice to music.

# Cha Cha Beginners Side Basic (Latin)

There is a YouTube video https://youtu.be/m7DGfEN_H7M that fits with this lesson plan. The numbered sections of the video and this lesson plan match to make working with both easier. For most students I recommend watching the video and regularly pausing (and maybe rewinding) as you also read this lesson plan. However, depending on your learning style, you might develop a better approach for you. Note, the video is designed so you can join in using a smaller space such as your living room.

## Section A: Introduction

### 1. Do the Complete Beginners Lesson First

*(Students I see repeating the earlier lessons tend to do better.)*

If you are diving into this lesson but are still not too confident with the earlier ones I recommend going back and repeating an earlier one instead.

Further Ideas: I always seem to be fighting my students over the lessons going too fast or too slow! I generally try to get a feeling for the majority of my class and accept that some people will find it "too fun" or "too technical" and stop coming (or worse keep coming but keep complaining). My personal challenge as a teacher is to teach in such a way that a wide range of learning preferences are catered for. But I always find some people don't like it and if they start to moan a lot I will remind them it is a group class and that they can always book private lessons.

## Section B: Warm Up

There is no suggested warm up for this lesson so you might find your own to do. Perhaps dance to a song or find something from a previous lesson to repeat.

## Section C: New Skills

### 2. Watch and Copy Side Basic

*(Join in or just watch this demonstration of side basic.)*

I recommend replaying this as many times as you need to. Get a feeling for what the move is and try joining in. Keep stopping and starting as much as you need to.

Further Ideas: Stepping sideways can lead a beginner to drift their standing leg sideways as well. I find emphasising the piece of paper helps.

### 3. Back Basic Side-by-Side

*(Join in with dancing the back basic steps side-by-side.)*

In preparation for learning side basic we recap the leader and follower back basic steps.

Further Ideas: I am mainly including this so the viewer can get used to how the demonstration works.

### 4. Side Basic Side-by-Side

*(Join in with dancing the side basic steps side-by-side.)*

We dance the leader and follower steps at the same time. Just like with back basic these are mirror steps.

Further Ideas: I am doing this side-by-side in the video. In a class in a room I might just arrange everyone on each side of the room or possibly skip this completely.

### 5. Side Basic Feet Positions

*(When to move sideways and when to stay on the piece of paper.)*

Only the first step is off the piece of paper.

Further Ideas: This is a common question and/or problem for dancers new to this basic step.

### 6. Side Basic Together

*(Dance side basic together.)*

Now we have got the steps sorted it is time to dance together.

Further Ideas: As always, I find dancing in couples fixes so many things. I will encourage my students to look down if it helps but look up as soon as they can. (I have met teachers that do not allow students to look down at all but I find that if I give "permission" they seem not to do it very much.) If you are teaching and the class is struggling with the new basic step, I find that jumping ahead to the "dancing together" exercises can often make it easier (I think this is at least partly because they have the "tactile learning" of feeling what their partner is doing).

### 7. Sideways Step Overcommit Problem

*(Staying centred will help this move work better.)*

The sideways step is only with one foot while the other foot stays behind. This can mean not moving completely sideways.

Further Ideas: I would only do this exercise with a particular class if it looked like it would help their particular needs.

## Section D: Dance Naturally

### 8. Continuous Practice

*(Dance continually to a song.)*

A chance to repeat the move over and over to help remember it and make it feel more natural.

Further Ideas: In a "real life" class I would put the music on and force myself to do nothing. I find that after typically 20 seconds even classes not familiar with my teaching style will realise I am not going to help and start dancing on their own (and remember some will find hearing the rhythm easier, start sooner, and so give a model for others to copy which is fine and how I see it work on a social dance floor). I want them to have the chance to practice all the elements they will need for social dancing including starting on their own. In class I often talk about tips for this (for people who find it difficult) including watching someone else (who seems to be a good dancer) to get reminders of what to do.

# Cha Cha Beginners New Yorkers (Latin)

There is a YouTube video https://youtu.be/dJRasl1_OBE that fits with this lesson plan. The numbered sections of the video and this lesson plan match to make working with both easier. For most students I recommend watching the video and regularly pausing (and maybe rewinding) as you also read this lesson plan. However, depending on your learning style, you might develop a better approach for you. Note, the video is designed so you can join in using a smaller space such as your living room.

## Section A: Introduction

### 1. Sort-of a Basic Step

*(This is either a basic step or a move or something else.)*

I think you could call this a basic step. It is similar to other basic steps in that it uses a piece of paper and you step off the piece of paper only the first step. However, typically dancers do not do this move for long periods of time so in that sense it is more of a "move".

Further Ideas: Yes I do use the words "basic step" a lot. That is a phrase I like as it is a common one and I like the idea you can keep doing it over and over. If I could reinvent partner dancing from the ground up I would change the name as I think the word "basic" is unfortunate and I am endlessly dealing with students who want to "go beyond the basics". In reality if you watch me (and other experienced dancers) dance socially I will often do a "basic step" for long periods of time during which the dancing can look very nice and myself and my partner enjoy it. Plus, it seems demoralising to me for students to hear they are doing a "basic step". But, this phrase is in common usage and I prefer to stick with the same language other teachers use to make learning an easier experience for the many students who learn with more than one teacher.

## Section B: Warm Up

As there is not warm up for this video you could add your own by dancing for a song or picking out something from a previous lesson to repeat.

## Section C: New Skills

### 2. Watch and Copy New Yorkers

*(Join in or just watch this demonstration of New Yorkers.)*

I recommend replaying this as many times as you need to. Get a feeling for what the move is and try joining in. Keep stopping and starting as much as you need to.

Further Ideas: In my experience the key thing is stepping through with the correct foot. It needs to be the foot on the other side (compared to the direction you are going) which can be confusing for some people.

### 3. Step Across

*(You need to step across on the first beat of each bar.)*

This is an unusual move because you are stepping with the foot on the opposite side to which you are going. This is difficult to talk about but I have exaggerated the demonstration to try to make it clear.

Further Ideas: This is often an issue for new learners of this move.

### 4. Only the First Step is off the Piece of Paper

*(I find students like this to be clarified.)*

Of the three steps, only the first one is off the piece of paper. Note that because of the turning of the body the "on the piece of paper" steps may not be exactly on the piece of paper because otherwise you could twist a knee (and anyway as usual don't copy exactly and do what feels comfortable to you).

Further Ideas: This is the kind of place where as a less experienced teacher I might have talked a lot and explained it different ways. I now instead state it very clearly once. I think a small percentage of students benefit from multiple verbal explanations. In my experience (1) more students are confused by too much verbal instructions (compared to those who benefit) and (2) regardless in most cases I think verbalising less is better in dance teaching. However, an important point is that I talk a lot during some practice exercises and will say at the start of those exercises "I'm going to talk a lot during this exercise for the benefit of people who like to learn from spoken explanations but you can just ignore what I am saying and do the exercise if you want". By combining talking with an exercise I would do anyway the verbal learners benefit without it being boring for other students. Remember also that I allow students to not join in with exercises if they wish and in a situation like this some verbal learners simply stand and watch and listen.

### 5. New Yorkers Side-by-Side

*(Join in with dancing the New Yorkers side-by-side.)*

We dance the leader and follower steps at the same time. The steps are mirror versions of what your partner is doing.

Further Ideas: I am doing this side-by-side in the video. In a class in a room I might just arrange leaders on one side of the room and followers on the other or in most cases I think I would skip this completely.

### 6. New Yorkers Together

*(Dance New Yorkers together.)*

Now we have got the steps sorted hopefully we can dance it together!

Further Ideas: I find the inner voice of many students while learning New Yorkers is often saying "partner dancing is always symmetrical and this looks wrong". I try to look out for this problem and remind my students that this is a different shape and to expect it to look unusual.

### 7. New Yorkers Together Holding Hands

*(Dancing New Yorkers without letting go of the hands.)*

Holding on with both hands makes New Yorkers more difficult for most people because it holds you back from stepping through so far.

Further Ideas: This is an optional extra that I like to include as a way to draw attention to the hands while also teaching something else useful.

### 8. What to do With The Hands

*(You have options.)*

(1) You might not hold hands at all if that is easier. (2) Or just hold in the centre, letting go with the "outside hands". (3) Or hold hands all the time which I personally like as a variation but beware that many people will tell you that you are doing it "wrong" if you do this socially.

Further Ideas: I might spend longer on this in a class I am teaching. This is somewhere that I might get students to share their favourites and why. I do not like doing this "sharing" too much in dancing classes as I like my dance classes to get on with the physical learning but this feels like a good place to do it. Perhaps it is a good place to talk about personal preferences because it is generally difficult to lead and that helps address that.

### 9. How to Lead New Yorkers

*(Carefully!)*

For beginners I suggest just telling your partner. Leading this can be a dangerous if done too strongly as you are leading a twist motion which is what often results in injuries. However, just so you know, many experienced leaders use the hand that is holding on in the middle to push through and indicate the "opening out" shape.

Further Ideas: (1) I am not covering this in detail in the video mainly because I cannot monitor the lead strength of the person watching (and also observe whether followers are prepared for the move and not being surprised) and don't want to encourage anything dangerous. With a "real life" class I could spend time on this. As usual, this video lesson is actually something I would do in maybe 10 minutes as only one part of a lesson and then return to in future lessons. This allows the skill to develop naturally over the course of a few lessons rather than forcing it during one lesson. (I might often spend a whole lesson on a very specific dancing skill with advanced dancers but rarely with beginners). (2) I don't always lead with a push through the centre. It seems to be the most common lead I've noticed others do but you can also use a "space lead" or "momentum lead".

## Section D: Dance Naturally

### 10. New Yorkers Together

*(Repeat of previous exercise.)*

To start "dancing naturally" we simply repeat the whole thing. You can do your hands however you like.

Further Ideas: As usual, in a "real life" class I would put music on and let the students practice in their own way. With something like this I would encourage them to take breaks and restart or do other basic steps as well for variety. I think doing New Yorkers over and over would get tiring and mean most people would either struggle and maybe start "reinforcing mistakes" or get the hang of it and get bored.

# Cha Cha Beginners Criss Cross Basic (Latin)

There is a YouTube video https://youtu.be/Rebk2IMeukI that fits with this lesson plan. The numbered sections of the video and this lesson plan match to make working with both easier. For most students I recommend watching the video and regularly pausing (and maybe rewinding) as you also read this lesson plan. However, depending on your learning style, you might develop a better approach for you. Note, the video is designed so you can join in using a smaller space such as your living room.

## Section A: Introduction

### 1. This is Asymmetrical

*(The shapes we dance in this lesson are not symmetrical.)*

Depending on your personal learning style, this lesson could be a really easy or really difficult. I find students who really try to focus on the instructions of the lesson and are methodical find it easier: I think this is because it is so different to previous lessons that you have to treat it as learning a new thing and really concentrate.

Further Ideas: The most common mistake I see is people doing something like New Yorkers (or a similar pattern) as they try to become symmetrical with their partner. My teaching approach is not to talk about this but just keep saying "this is a new and different move so let it feel different". A trick I like is to get the follower doing back basic with their eyes closed and I join in as leader doing cross basic: I then get the follower to open their eyes and I say "this is what it should look and feel like".

### 2. Keep Retrying Exercises

*(The video that goes with this lesson is designed for you to keep going back to retry things.)*

This is a very new shape compared to the previous lessons. It is very natural for students to need extra practice time to get used to it. As usual, instead of making the accompanying video very long I have simply left it up to you to keep going back and retrying exercises again as you need to. One option would be to keep coming back to the video every couple of days to slowly get used to this alternative overall pattern for latin dancing.

## Section B: Warm Up

### 3. Back Basic Side-by-Side

*(Join in with dancing the back basic steps side-by-side.)*

In preparation for learning the criss cross basic we recap the leader and follower back basic steps.

Further Ideas: I am mainly including this so the viewer can get used to how the demonstration works.

## Section C: New Skills

### 4. Watch and Copy Cross Basic

*(Join in or just watch this demonstration of criss cross basic.)*

I recommend replaying this in the video as many times as you need to. Get a feeling for what the move is and try joining in. Keep stopping and starting as much as you need to.

Further Ideas: This is almost an exact copy of back basic but stepping forwards instead of backwards.

### 5. Actually Step Across

*(The first step of every bar is across the standing foot.)*

This can be difficult to talk about but here is a demonstration of what the first step should look and feel like.

Further Ideas: I find this is crucial and that the majority of errors are because the student does not step across. Fundamentally this is about stepping with the next available foot. (To reword the previous sentence, "fundamentally this is about stepping with alternating feet every beat".)

### 6. Criss Cross Basic Side-by-Side (Leader Forwards)

*(Join in with dancing the criss cross basic steps side-by-side.)*

We dance the leader and follower steps at the same time. As the leader steps across the follower steps backwards. You will both be sending your foot in approximately the same direction (perhaps towards the corner of the room depending on where you are dancing).

Further Ideas: I am doing this side-by-side in the video. In a class in a room I might just arrange everyone on each side of the room or possibly skip this completely.

### 7. Criss Cross Basic Together (Leader Forwards)

*(Dance criss cross basic together.)*

Now we have got the steps sorted hopefully we can dance it together without stepping on each other's feet too much!

Further Ideas: If this does not work I usually try reminding the student about it not being symmetrical. If that does not work I might jump in and lead (fairly strongly) the person stepping the wrong way (or both students if necessary). If that does not work I will go back to teaching the individual steps carefully again. I find the criss cross basic can be very problematic for some people to learn so I do not like to struggle too much if it is not quite working and instead do some more warming up and basic skill work before trying again. Note, this exercise would be an "extended practice to music" for my students in a typical class and I would go around helping.

### 8. Only One Person Steps Across (Discussion)

*(The other person steps backwards.)*

The idea that one person steps across and one person steps backwards is demonstrated. You can join in obviously.

Further Ideas: I find two big issues in learning this. The first is that even if the leader is strongly leading the follower to step backwards they often resist it. This is often because beginner dancers have not yet learnt to follow, maybe because beginner leaders are not yet leading very well so they are (quite sensibly in my opinion) pro-active and try to work things out as well as just follow. The second issue is that many people have a preconceived idea that dancing should be symmetrical but it does not have to be with this move being an example. So, highlighting that it is not symmetrical can help.

### 9. Criss Cross Basic Side-by-Side (Leader Backwards)

*(Join in with dancing the criss cross basic steps side-by-side.)*

We dance the leader and follower steps at the same time. As the leader steps backwards the follower steps across.

Further Ideas: I am doing this side-by-side in the video. In a class in a room I might just arrange everyone on each side of the room or possibly skip this completely.

### 10. Criss Cross Basic Together (Leader Backwards)

*(Dance criss cross basic together.)*

Now we have got the steps sorted hopefully we can dance it together without stepping on each other's feet too much! Oh, and yes this is different from "criss cross basic (leader forwards)" which we did earlier.

Further Ideas: In "real life" class I would typically instead give extended "practice time" and go around helping.

### 11. Criss Cross Basic Together (Leader Forwards Repeat)

*(Dance criss cross basic together.)*

Now we can try the other version again.

Further Ideas: This can be a big problem in a lesson. I would normally only teach one version and then teach the other one in another class. Only for this self-learning resource (where I think there is an implicit understanding that the students using the resource will "manage their own learning" more) have I included both versions in the same lesson.

### 12. Shape of the First Step

*(The first step is crucial in setting the pattern of this basic step.)*

As long as you either step across or backwards and then carry on doing the same, the move works. So, here is extra practice at working out the correct direction for the first step.

Further Ideas: This is a common problem and I often find students will be able to do criss cross basic and then later suddenly get confused as they start looking at it more carefully and changing it a bit. Most of the time I find it is because there is a desire to make the move look symmetrical. This is not a symmetrical move. Also, I find with my students that if the follower looks down for a clue that in most situations they can get some help (I encourage students to do this a little bit as a self-learning technique) but for criss cross basic I think looking down is very unhelpful.

### 13. Steps 2 and 3 are on the Piece of Paper

*(We are still dancing "off and back onto the piece of paper".)*

Just like with most of the other basic steps, only the first step is off the piece of paper. The second and third steps are on the piece of paper. Because there is some twisting happening I do not generally recommend going exactly onto the piece of paper as it could be uncomfortable and I don't usually see people dance like that anyway.

Further Ideas: I often talk about this earlier in class (often talking about it while we do an exercise so people are not stood around listening) but because of the self-learning format I decided to hold it back until towards the end for its own section.

### 14. Why is This Lesson Called Criss-Cross Basic But You Keep Saying Cross Basic?

*(One is a single person dancing, the other is two people dancing.)*

Cross basic is what I call the move where you step forwards every first beat. Criss-cross basic is what I call it when one person is doing back basic and the other is doing cross basic.

## Section D: Dance Naturally

### 15. Continuous Practice of the Two Versions

*(Dance each of the versions of criss-cross basic.)*

This is extended practice time to help make the move more comfortable.

Further Ideas: As usual, this would not be a led exercise in one of my classes but a practice time with me going around and giving individual help.

### Extra Note For Teachers

*(Leading this basic step.)*

Further Ideas: There is a way for the leader to lead this. It involves "dissociating" their upper and lower body. I would typically teach this by first getting the leader to stand still and lead the follower in back basic (the leader must stand still during this). Then the full challenge is still to lead the follower into back basic with the upper body but do the cross basic with the lower body at the same time. I have not included this in the video as I think it is too complex and too dangerous for students (who are not being monitored by a teacher) for self-learning.

# Latin Solo Practice

Students are often keen to practise on their own to get better faster. I mainly recommend:

Listening to music to get more familiar with the rhythm and timing.

Drilling the basic step so it becomes better part of your "muscle memory". I can do most of the basic steps whilst thinking about something else because it is so instinctive. However, I recommend doing the practice to music so you are not developing muscle memory with the wrong timing.

Watching demonstration dances and trying to spot what is going on. Can you see which basic steps they are dancing? Can you see which moves they are doing? Are they always in time? Is their footwork continually the same?

There are 4 lessons in this book covering solo practice for latin:

Latin Beginners Follower Solo Practice
Latin Beginners Leader Solo Practice
Latin Improvers Follower Solo Practice
Latin Improvers Leader Solo Practice

# Latin Beginners Follower Solo Practice

There is a YouTube video https://youtu.be/_s0YtEkolGw that fits with this lesson plan. The numbered sections of the video and this lesson plan match to make working with both easier. For most students I recommend watching the video and regularly pausing (and maybe rewinding) as you also read this lesson plan. However, depending on your learning style, you might develop a better approach for you. Note, the video is designed so you can join in using a smaller space such as your living room.

## Section A: Introduction

### 1. I am Dancing Follower Steps

*(I am dancing follower steps in the video for you to copy.)*

Unless I say otherwise simply copy what I am doing. I am not dancing leader in the video, I am dancing follower steps so we can all do the same thing. This lesson uses salsa so if that is still too difficult for you then I recommend repeating (for example) the complete beginner rumba lesson instead.

Further Ideas: In a group class I occasionally remind people that they can "join in or watch or do your own thing". If someone is doing something different from the rest of the class (and not being a big distraction to other students) then this is fine and if it feels right I might go and speak to them later to see if there is anything they'd like done differently in my teaching (which may not be possible but I can at least ask.).

### 2. Stop and Start Again

*(Something you can do to improve your own learning. I have not included one of these exercises in this lesson because you can make it up yourself as you join in.)*

I strongly encourage you to keep trying these exercises as much as you like to make the basics feel more natural and easy. I also encourage you to stop and start again (actually "stop and join back in" if you are doing an exercise led by me as we mainly do in this lesson) even if you don't think you need to. I have found students who keep stopping and starting develop better timing and generally become better dancers. I think one reason is that stopping and starting disrupts your flow and is harder than just continuing: So it is a way of doing "more difficult practice" so that normal dancing then feels easier. I think another reason is that you are developing a specific skill of "picking back up if you get lost" which definitely is something I have to do a lot in my dancing even if as an advanced dancer I don't actually stop but simply disguise that I got lost by sneakily drifting back into time.

Further Ideas: I use stop and start so much as a teacher! I find it is a way to improve almost anyone's dancing. With advanced dancers I still do it, for example I'll shout stop in the middle of a complex move and then get everyone to hold the position and then continue from where we left off: And while we are paused I might encourage a discussion of our options from this position.

## Section B: Warm Up

There is no warm up section in the accompanying video. It is presumed that you have already done some beginner lessons before doing this and I think the skill exercises are (for most people) gentle enough to act as a warm up on their own.

## Section C: New Skills

### 3. On-the-Spot Basic Practice (Salsa)

*(A nice exercise for emphasising the role of the feet.)*

Let's dance the latin rhythm on the spot. I find this more difficult than something like back basic (and many other people do as well). However, I think it is a great "training basic step".

Further Ideas: I have had some people confidently claiming this exercise is a waste of time. I defend this basic step (which I have found many teachers never cover) by pointing out various things including (1) the fact it is a component of many advanced moves, (2) in advanced dancing the follower can help by dancing on the spot if there is no lead (neither a space lead nor a momentum lead nor a push lead) so it is a good "default basic" that I train my advanced followers to do if they are not led and (3) for beginners I find it can help many students understand the three steps better than the other basics where the movement off the spot can disguise the second step to the eye of an inexperienced dancer.

### 4. On-the-Spot Basic Practice (No Music) (Salsa)

*(This is a repeat of the previous exercise without music.)*

I recommend sometimes dancing without music (if you have at least one person with good timing to lead it). I find this helpful for many reasons including making it easier to keep going if you can't hear the rhythm in a particular song.

Further Ideas: I have seen cringe-worthy examples of teachers leading an exercise like this when their timing is off. It varies but typical consequences are students then dancing worse once the music is back on and/or some students getting very confused (generally not during the exercise but later when something else contradicts it). So, if you are a teacher you might try asking people (who will give you honest feedback) to confirm if they think you are dancing in time well enough to lead exercises without music.

### 5. Back Basic Practice (Salsa)

*(Now dance back-basic.)*

Many people find this easier than on-the-spot basic. Join in as I dance back basic.

Further Ideas: I exaggerate my stepping when I demonstrate this so that students who find it more difficult to "watch and copy" might find it easier.

### 6. Back Basic Practice (No Music) (Salsa)

*(Again dancing without music but a different basic step.)*

If you are led by someone who is dancing in time I think this is a useful exercise with any move.

Further Ideas: If you are a teacher then even if your dancing style is to make the third step late, I recommend trying to make it exactly on the beat so that beginners have something simpler to copy.

### 7. Back Basic Practice (Salsa)

*(Dance back basic to a salsa rhythm.)*

As well as practising dancing the back basic we also do some "stop starts" and I discuss some dancing topics as we go along.

Further Ideas: I often like to talk over exercises. The sections of a lesson where a teacher stands and talks to the class I like to do while also doing an exercise to save time and so that people who do not want to listen have something to do. (And don't get me started on forcing students to listen! I think if a student does not want to listen that is fine and if my lesson only works if they are really concentrating as I explain something in detail I consider my lesson to be badly designed.)

## 8. Back Basic Practice (Fast Salsa)

*(Dancing to a fast salsa can be very difficult so this is a challenging exercise.)*

More back basic practice including "stop starts" and general discussion.

Further Ideas: Dancing faster can help encourage you to take smaller steps which is an authentic styling for many types of latin dance. Many dancers find that being able to dance fast improves all their dancing although for others it can get them in the habit of going fast and they can then find dancing slower more difficult.

## 9. How to Help Your Leader

*(Partner dancing requires both a leader and a follower, so working together constructively is a good thing.)*

In this section of the video I discuss some issues relating to leaders and how it affects followers. I have seen some followers who will only dance with experienced dancers and do not like helping beginners. If everyone was like this I am not sure the hobby would grow very well as it would create problems for leaders when they either start out or are going through a learning period in their dancing. Fortunately many followers like to dance with beginners and also work constructively with them to help them improve. Many issues are discussed including the need to be patient and just do basic step while the leader works things out in their head and prepares to do the next move.

Further Ideas: Unfortunately this is something I regularly have to talk about in class. I try to remember to mention it at least once a month in class as sometimes the teacher is not aware of negative interactions happening between students. Leaders obviously also need to be aware of followers but at the early stages of learning it is often the leader with the most to learn and therefore who needs the most understanding from their partner.

## Section D: Dance Naturally

There is no "dancing naturally" section for this lesson. The reason is that this is all about practising and polishing existing skills. There is not really a take-away core set of skills and the learner is encouraged to push themselves to be as good as they personally want to be.

# Latin Beginners Leader Solo Practice

There is a YouTube video https://youtu.be/05YLGx1240k that fits with this lesson plan. The numbered sections of the video and this lesson plan match to make working with both easier. For most students I recommend watching the video and regularly pausing (and maybe rewinding) as you also read this lesson plan. However, depending on your learning style, you might develop a better approach for you. Note, the video is designed so you can join in using a smaller space such as your living room.

## Section A: Introduction

### 1. This is Fairly Fast Practice

*(This might be too fast if you are just starting out.)*

This video is for anyone learning latin dancing. It is particularly aimed at beginner leaders. This lesson uses salsa so if that is still too difficult for you then I recommend repeating (for example) the complete beginners rumba lesson instead. At any time you can "stop and start again" or "stop and join back in" if you get lost or if something simply feels odd: I recommend this instead of trying to fix it as you dance because stopping helps prevent "bad muscle memory" and has other benefits as well.

Further Ideas: I like to have lesson plans like this in reserve in case I get mainly leaders turning up to a class one evening.

## Section B: Warm Up

There is no "warm up" section for this video but I think the first skills exercise doubles up as a warm up for most people (but you might want a slower, more gentle warm up).

## Section C: New Skills

### 2. Salsa Continuous Practice

*(Get going dancing with me demonstrating.)*

I dance salsa and you can join in or watch or do something else. What "something else" might people do? Well, some people like to try and do a different basic step and see if they can stay in time with me.

Further Ideas: After years of feedback from students I resist the temptation to do anything but start with a warm up and repetition of previous things. My students have "real lives" outside of class and might have spent the week between classes stressed and with no time to practice: This is the reality so I make my teaching fit with this need.

### 3. Salsa Stop Start Practice

*(We dance but keep stopping and starting again!)*

Join in as I dance salsa but keep stopping. We "freeze in place" during the stop and then start again immediately. So, for example we do not "change our position" or "change our feet" or "move so we are more comfortable" while waiting to start again.

Further Ideas: I find this to be a very effective teaching technique and could go on about it for hours. There are so many benefits including students seeing the shape and position during the stop which otherwise passes in a fleeting moment.

### 4. Salsa Medium-Fast Continuous Practice

*(We speed up!)*

Dancing to faster music is a fairly essential skill for social dancing, although this depends on the music played at the venues you go to. I find students who only learn to slower music usually struggle if the music is faster at a social event.

Further Ideas: Over the years I have started introducing this sooner and sooner with my beginners. I now believe that even if they cannot do it the exercise builds the awareness that this is what they are aiming for and they will adapt their learning with this in mind: The alternative of saying "we are 12 weeks into learning and actually this is how fast you need to be dancing" can be a shocking reveal for students (who might think "well I could do that before but I adjusted how I danced because I thought it was supposed to be slower").

### 5. Breaking Down the Back Basic

*(A look at the basic step and how it works.)*

I briefly demonstrate the basic step. Then break down the stepping. This is an unusually "talky" way of teaching for me but I will occasionally drop in something like this to give a different perspective.

Further Ideas: This is particularly designed for the video. It is a summary of the basic step intended to help the viewer manage their own learning. If not teaching via a video I would try to choose more specifically the appropriate exercise for the needs of the moment and the students.

### 6. Changing Between Back Basic and On-the-Spot Basic (Rumba)

*(Mainly back basic with some on-the-spot basic mixed in.)*

For a beginner leader the more confident you can be changing from one step to the next the better. Here is an exercise combining more practice of back basic with changing between that and on-the-spot basic.

Further Ideas: This can feel slow for teachers if they forget what it is like to be a beginner. I find most beginners appreciate the extra practice of the basics and the chance to start working on changing on the left. If it is too easy then I start pushing the student by using faster changes and starting to mix in different basic steps. This lesson is fairly short but if I were to extend it to be a longer lesson I would likely add in a lot more different basic steps to practise changing between.

## Section D: Dance Naturally

There is no "dancing naturally" section for this lesson. The reason is that this is all about practising and polishing existing skills. There is not really a take-away core set of skills and the viewer is encouraged to push themselves to be as good as they personally want to be.

# Latin Improvers Follower Solo Practice

There is a YouTube video https://youtu.be/qUYEnhZqqb0 that fits with this lesson plan. The numbered sections of the video and this lesson plan match to make working with both easier. For most students I recommend watching the video and regularly pausing (and maybe rewinding) as you also read this lesson plan. However, depending on your learning style, you might develop a better approach for you. Note, the video is designed so you can join in using a smaller space such as your living room.

## Section A: Introduction

### 1. I am Dancing Follower Steps

*(I am dancing follower steps in this video for you to copy.)*

Unless I say otherwise simply copy what I am doing. I am not dancing leader in this video. I am dancing follower steps so we can all do the same thing.

Further Ideas: I get frustrated by teachers who get frustrated with students who are confused by this. If you are learning to dance, especially as an adult, you may have a stressful life and be very tired. So, a student might easily forget that I am dancing the follower steps.

## Section B: Warm Up

There is no "warm up" section for this video. It is presumed that you have already done some improver videos before doing this improver video and the first skill exercise acts as a warm up (for most students although you might feel the need for a more gentle warm up).

## Section C: New Skills

### 2. Basic Step Recap for Forward-and-Back Basic

*(A look at the basic step and how it works.)*

I briefly demonstrate the basic step. Then break down the stepping. Then I do extended practice to music for you to join in with.

Further Ideas: This is particularly for the video. It is a summary of the basic step intended to help the viewer manage their own learning. If not teaching via a video I would try to choose more specifically the appropriate exercise for the needs of the moment and the students. In class I would sometimes pick a basic step (I have picked forward-and-back for this lesson plan because it is used as the "second one to learn" within the overall learning progression for this series of lessons and so it is a likely place for a learner to have problems) to focus on in more detail if it felt useful: However I rarely teach like this.

### 3. Change Between Different Steps (Salsa)

*(Dance and change between different basic steps.)*

If you can change naturally between all the different basic steps then you have a good variety to your dancing that you can use in combination. Usually the leader is making the decisions about which steps to do. If you are used to changing between basic steps this can make following easier.

Further Ideas: The reason I originally developed this type of exercise was to get the follower to be balanced and waiting during the 4th beat ready to go in any direction. If you are used to the idea you might go in any direction then I have found that the tendency to anticipate is reduced.

### 4. Change Between Different Steps (Cha Cha)

*(Dance and change between different basic steps.)*

In cha cha the speed of the quick steps on during beats 3 and 4 (assuming you are dancing on the 1) can make it more difficult to be balanced and ready for the lead at the start of the next bar. So, if this exercise is more difficult than the same exercise with another dance that might be why.

Further Ideas: My personal experience is that an exercise like this is easiest with rumba, medium-difficult with salsa and most difficult with cha cha.

### 5. Follow the Hands Exercise

*(Practice following the leader's hands and not the leader's own movement.)*

There are different ways of leading. In this section of the video I lead using my hands. The idea is that you copy the movement of my hands with your whole body. For example, if I step backwards you might step forwards or you might step backwards (or something else) and the way to know is by ignoring my feet and focussing on my hands.

Further Ideas: I will do this type of exercise with a whole class getting them to copy me.

### 6. Delaying the Third Step

*(Delaying the third step is an alternative styling option.)*

I do not generally recommend this alternative styling to beginners or even improvers. I think there are more important things to work on for most dancers and it can confuse beginner or improver leaders who will often look down to check which foot you are on. However, I feel it is worth mentioning because it is a fairly common way to dance and you might find it easier. You may hear of this or alternative options described as "the correct way to dance latin" but I would not be so bold as to claim which is universally correct.

Further Ideas: It is important to me to represent alternative approaches and not bias towards only those that I like. This is an example of something I do like and mix into my own dancing sometimes.

### 7. Styling Dilemma

*(Styling is good and bad!)*

As a follower you can add styling. Perhaps you might take the third step late to create a nice interplay/dynamic with the music. Perhaps you might do graceful movements with your hands/arms. Perhaps you might pose a bit and have fun with the shapes in the dance. However! When you do this it will often make it more difficult for the leader to lead the dance. It can make the position of your hand (which the leader might want) unpredictable. It can make an advanced move that requires you to be led into an extra step after the third beat difficult/impossible. It can make very fast sequences of moves problematic as the styling can take time out of the dancing which an advanced leader might want to use for more fancy moves or lead preparation or driving you into extra steps to make very complex moves possible. What to do!? I recommend a flexible approach. I find the followers I dance best with often do no styling initially but then after a while start putting some in once they get a feeling for where my dancing is giving them space and time.

Further Ideas: I think the biggest problem I have with this is communicating just how rapidly a good leader can put together a sequence of moves. With a good follower doing minimal styling I can sometimes lead a sequence of 20 or more moves, each taking a maximum of 4 beats and with no recovery time between them. I simply cannot do this if the following is not really tight and "boring". However, my partners usually agree it is worth "having boring stepping" for the experience of such an "interesting intensity of spins and rapid position changes and drops" in such a short space of time. Want to burn the dance floor with a whirl of moves? Then drop the styling so I can use every millisecond to build up the momentum and intensity of the dance! But, I don't dance like this all the time and obviously if my partner likes styling that's great and I'll probably do some solo dancing too.

## Section D: Dance Naturally

There is no "dancing naturally" section for this video. The reason is that this is all about practising and polishing existing skills. There is not really a take-away core set of skills and the viewer is encouraged to push themselves to be as good as they personally want to be.

# Latin Improvers Leader Solo Practice

There is a YouTube video https://youtu.be/HxCZisFRXHU that fits with this lesson plan. The numbered sections of the video and this lesson plan match to make working with both easier. For most students I recommend watching the video and regularly pausing (and maybe rewinding) as you also read this lesson plan. However, depending on your learning style, you might develop a better approach for you. Note, the video is designed so you can join in using a smaller space such as your living room.

## Section A: Introduction

### 1. A Mixture of Exercises

*(This lesson has various things, some of which you may find useful to your needs.)*

I think this is one of the more difficult things to make a lesson on. It is simply a recap and extended practice of things already covered in other lesson. I think practice like this is vital to become a better dancer but you might find some exercises in this lesson are not useful for you.

Further Ideas: The exercises in this lesson include examples of what I might do for a warm up for an improver class or during a private lesson with a leader.

### 2. Side Basic Can Vary

*(Yes there are different types of side basic.)*

I teach at least two different types of side basic which I call "side basic" and "travelling side basic" and there are others as well. In this video I use "side basic". This can be confusing but simply watch carefully and hopefully you'll be ok!

Further Ideas: This is an example of how there are different moves which can look similar. I try as a teacher to be understanding of students bringing other moves from other teachers and if something works I may point out they are doing it differently to how I am teaching but quickly say that if they want they can continue the way they are. Sometimes they will say they know but they are trying some variations: I know that as a student I have often had teachers come and "correct me" when I was merely trying something different after having practised the move we had been given a few times. So, as a teacher I try to help my students as a "peer" not a "teacher" at least until I get to know them.

## Section B: Warm Up

There is no "warm up" section for this lesson. It is presumed that you have already done some improver videos before doing this improver video. The skill exercises are not too intensive to begin with and therefore act as their own warm up (although you might want to do something more gentle to warm up).

## Section 3: Skills

### 3. Forward-and-Back Basic Step Breakdown

*(The individual steps are broken down slowly.)*

Some people find this useful for their particular learning style.

Further Ideas: This is particularly included because this is a self-learning resource. In a typical "real life" class I will watch the students and only do this if it seems necessary. Obviously a teacher could do this with any of the basic steps, I happen to have chosen forward-and-back basic for this lesson.

### 4. Change Between Different Steps on the Left (Rumba)

*(Dance and change between different basic steps.)*

If you can change naturally between all the different basic steps then you have a good variety to draw on in your dancing. I found that once I could do this I had a basic pattern that I could keep dancing and which I could then add other moves on top of.

Further Ideas: The reason for changing on the left is that it gives the follower more time to respond. The side basic, back basic, on-the-spot basic and forward-and-back basic all have a similar step on the right for the follower at the point where the leader is stepping with their left. If the follower does not pick up on the first step what the basic step is then the dance will still work and they have 4 more beats during which it should become obvious what the leader intended. The only real problem here is the New Yorker and the criss-cross basic where the follower comes forwards and these two basic steps are often the most difficult for improver dancers.

### 5. Change Between Different Steps on the Left (Salsa)

*(Same exercise as for the rumba.)*

Trying the same exercises to faster music typically makes it more difficult. The only time I find a student finds it easier is with some very "intuitive" dancers who find it difficult to relax unless the music is fast.

### 6. Standing Still While the Follower Dances

*(Leading but not dancing.)*

If you are practising with a follower a good exercise can be to dance together and for you to then stop while the follower keeps going: Then join back in. And repeat. You can keep doing this. An advanced version I actually use as a variation for social dancing is to lead the follower through a series of moves and not dance at all myself except to slow step around as necessary to keep up with them: This is a style of dancing that some leaders use a lot.

## Section D: Dance Naturally

There is no "dancing naturally" section for this lesson. The reason is that this is all about practising and polishing existing skills. There is not really a take-away core set of skills and the viewer is encouraged to push themselves to be as good as they personally want to be.

# Latin Improvers Cross Body Move

There is a YouTube video https://youtu.be/cfA3hJLR9c8 that fits with this lesson plan. The numbered sections of the video and this lesson plan match to make working with both easier. For most students I recommend watching the video and regularly pausing (and maybe rewinding) as you also read this lesson plan. However, depending on your learning style, you might develop a better approach for you. Note, the video is designed so you can join in using a smaller space such as your living room.

My experience is that most people find the cross body move is easiest to dance in rumba and then find they can do it in salsa after a few practice sessions and finally in cha cha after a few more.

## Section 1: Introduction

### 1. You Will Be Swapping Position With Your Partner

*(The cross body move is a way for the leader and follower to swap positions.)*

The cross body move is also called the cross body lead and has other names as well. I have often seen it abbreviated as CBM. This can be useful on a crowded dance floor to switch positions. In this lesson we dance it in a straight line which I like to do in class because I think it makes it easier to learn. You can then dance it differently if you like.

Further Ideas: This is definitely a skill where I like to explain it first. The idea of swapping sides seems to help a lot of people as it gives an easy way to remember the overall shape of the move. Also, the reason I think learning in a straight line is easier is because it makes it easier to watch and copy and not because I think the actual move is easier once learnt that way.

### 2. Left and Right Are Very Important in the Cross Body Move

*(You need to be on the correct foot or the move does not work.)*

You need to be on the same foot as the demonstration couple if you are joining in with an exercise for the cross body move. You may find yourself stopping and starting again a lot more often because of this. If you are part-way through and realise you are on the wrong foot simply stop and start again because I can basically guarantee it will not work and will mess up your "muscle memory" if you continue.

Further Ideas: This is one of the reasons I teach the cross body move in forward-and-back basic because this already gives us a clear difference between the stepping on each side.

## Section 2: Warm Up

### 3. Recap Forward-and-Back Basic

*(Dance with a partner doing forward-and-back basic.)*

The cross body move can be done anywhere but I like to first teach it in forward-and-back basic because they share a lot in common.

Further Ideas: You could also teach it from back-basic which can make it easier for some because the basic step and the move are then more different making it less likely they will get mixed up.

## Section 3: Skills

### 4. Look out for the Steps on the Spot

*(Always take three steps in a row even if you are not moving.)*

There is one place where the leader and one place where the follower will be stepping on the spot. Make sure you take that step or you will be out-of-time or out-of-step (depending on how you think about it) with your partner afterwards.

### 5. Leader Steps

*(We learn the leader steps individually.)*

The leader has to step out of the way. The follower will then be able to dance past. Followers might want to not join in with this exercise to avoid confusion.

Further Ideas: If you are a teacher with a large class it is possible to try and teach the leader and follower steps at the same time. However my personal experience is that instead teaching them separately means everyone gets to see the other person's steps which then helps later as they understand better what their partner has to do.

### 6. Leader Steps Broken Down Once

*(I briefly show the steps individually.)*

Step one is forwards, step two is to the side, step three is on the spot, step four is probably on the spot, steps five and six will be gently turning to face the new direction.

### 7. Follower Steps

*(We learn the follower steps individually.)*

The follower waits for the first three steps. Only once the leader is out of the way and the second set of beats start do we go forwards. Actually we should probably not even go forward then and instead wait to be led which might not happen if it is a different move that happens to start like a cross body move.

Further Ideas: Followers will often see the gap open up and want to go forwards early. If the follower does this it makes the move much less fun because then you lose the chance to really "burst forwards" or "dramatically accelerate". Most of my students agree that waiting means you can go through faster and have more fun.

### 8. Follower Steps Broken Down Twice

*(I briefly show the steps individually.)*

Steps one to three are no different than in basic step, step four is forwards, step five is beginning to turn and step six finishes the turn and is sort-of on the spot or backwards depending on your personal style.

### 9. Follower and Leader Steps Broken Down Together

*(We break down the follower steps and represent the position of the leader with a piece of paper and then with an actual leader.)*

This is particularly useful for the video as it means you can see even if the leader would have been standing in the way. It will help you see how the leader and follower steps fit together. We then repeat looking at the steps with me in the video which will hopefully get you even more used to what the dancing on the video looks like and how to copy it.

Further Ideas: In a "real life" class I will repeatedly use this approach of breaking things down if couples are getting confused. I find that cross body lead (unusually) benefits from working on the footwork a lot before bringing the move together.

### 10. Dance Together With no Hands

*(We dance the cross body move together with no hands.)*

Dancing with no hands is a good idea to begin with. Adding the hands will be done later when we will discover that there is a unique problem with the cross body move when holding hands. Leaders, now that we are dancing together you will need to wait for the follower to go past before turning to face them.

Further Ideas: In a "real life" class I will often leave it like this and then deal with the hands in a later lesson. For the purposes of this self-learning resource I think it makes sense to deal with the hands now.

### 11. Dance Together With no Hands (Extended Practice)

*(Same exercise repeated over and over.)*

This is an important point in the learning. Time for some extended practice.

## 12. Hands Are Important

*(The leader's left hand can accidentally pull the follower through.)*

I recommend that leaders let go with their left hand. This prevents accidentally pulling the follower through. As you get more experienced with the cross body move you can get more fancy with the hands but at this stage just letting go will make it work easily.

Further Ideas: There is an argument that I am teaching this with steps that are too large which is causing the hands to be a problem. However, for various technical reasons including making the demonstrations more accessible to all learners, helping students who need to initially learn with large steps and enabling people with not-such-good body awareness to still do the move, I am teaching it this way.

## 13. The Position of the Follower Halfway

*(Halfway through the cross body move the follower should not have gone too far.)*

This is a reminder that the follower should be patient and wait until the second half of the move to go forwards. This makes the move have a fast and dynamic ending which my students usually think is better.

Further Ideas: Some people sense the space around them and dance into it if they can. If you analyse most of the beginner moves, simply dancing into a space if you see it is not a problem. So, if you are a teacher I recommend you are understanding of any students who are prone to go forwards too early and give them plenty of time to adapt. Remember that if someone is not a verbal learner you may have to do something like put your arm in the way or step in the way yourself to make it really clear they should not be moving until the second half of the move.

## 14. Having a Break Halfway

*(A variation where the cross body move is split in two with forward-and-back basic in the middle.)*

I like to teach this mainly for two reasons. The first reason is that it encourages good leading and following. The second reason is that it helps split the cross body move into two parts which creates the opportunity for dancers to start using just the first or second half in their improvised dancing.

Further Ideas: I sometimes teach this first and only later show it can be finished straight away in just two bars. The benefit of doing this is that it immediately shows the leading and following better. The downside is that you are not exposing the class to the standard way of doing it first and their dancing can end up with unusual styling as students will often imprint with the first version they see.

## 15. Cross Body Move Every 4 Bars (Cha Cha)

*(Plenty of practice to a regular pattern.)*

To really interpret the music we don't want to be dancing to a regular pattern all the time. However, a regular pattern can be good for learning.

Further Ideas: Something like the cross body move is a regular set of steps. It is debatable whether something this structured should be taught. However, I teach cross body move because it is fairly common socially and seems to have become a key feature of latin dancing. I also like the move and think it is "variable enough" to allow for improvisational dancing anyway.

## 16. Aborted Cross Body Move

*(Dance the first half of the cross body move then don't finish it.)*

After the leader does the first three steps of the cross body move they then move back across without finishing the move. Continue with forward-and-back basic.

Further Ideas: This can be set as an individual practice exercise. The leader can either do this or finish the second half of the cross body move and see how well they can lead it. This challenges both the leader to lead well and the follower to follow well.

### 17. Continuous Cross Body Moves (Rumba)

*(A challenge to keep doing the move again and again.)*

Please don't get dizzy! Here is a challenge. As the cross body move gets easier you should find you can do it again and again as it takes up exactly two bars putting you back to where you started.

Further Ideas: This might feel easy if you are a teacher but if you have just learnt the move this gives very little recovery time between moves and can be very challenging.

### 18. Cross Body Move With Stops (Slow Salsa)

*(A chance to test your knowledge of the move with some unusual stops.)*

This exercise is a chance to test whether you can break in and out of the cross body move. If you become more advanced you are aiming to be able to use parts of this move at different points in your dancing rather than just always do the whole thing.

Further Ideas: Eventually as an advanced dancer you might be aiming to forget the move and just completely improvise every step. My experience is that this is possible but that the leader needs to be very good at letting go and feeling the moment and the follower has to be completely open to a different movement for every step.

### 19. How to Curve the Cross Body Move

*(Just so you know as it is fairly common.)*

Basically, the follower goes past the leader and then starts "orbiting around" the leader. It is as though the follower wants to keep going but is tied on a piece of string so can't go any further away and instead starts going around the leader. I have seen this style a lot and you might encounter it if you go social dancing.

Further Ideas: I have only included this in case you go social dancing in an area where the curved movement is regularly danced. I would normally save this for a while to avoid complicating things for any students who might have "barely understood" the lesson and who might get thrown by more explanation.

### 20. Running Away From Your Leader

*(This is something I teach to advanced students.)*

One styling option is for the follower to really go for it and go a long way past where the leader was originally standing. This essentially forces the leader to keep up. I would generally introduce this in advanced classes and I am mentioning it in this lesson for completeness.

Further Ideas: I sometimes do not mention this at all to a particular class. However, if the class are being very "rigid" and/or "understated" in their dancing I am more likely to cover this to try and "loosen them up". I find this exercise can bring dynamism into this potentially exciting move. However, I encourage the leaders to keep up (and for the followers to be sympathetic to the leader and not go too far if the leader has mobility problems) because if the couple simply separate I am not sure it is stylistically salsa any more (perhaps more resembling modern jive). Also, remember they still need to only take three steps per bar and complete the move in the usual number of steps.

## Section 4: Dance Naturally

### 21. Cross Body Move Every 2 Bars (Salsa)

*(A repetition exercise for learning.)*

Join in or watch or do your own thing as we do this practice exercise. Two bars of forward-and-back basic followed by the cross body move.

Further Ideas: Another regular pattern to get the move really comfortable before we start improvising more.

# Latin Improvers One or Two

There is a YouTube video https://youtu.be/GlLu4vj1TAY that fits with this lesson plan. The numbered sections of the video and this lesson plan match to make working with both easier. For most students I recommend watching the video and regularly pausing (and maybe rewinding) as you also read this lesson plan. However, depending on your learning style, you might develop a better approach for you. Note, the video is designed so you can join in using a smaller space such as your living room.

## Section A: Introduction

### 1. Discussion

*(A fairly long discussion of how to dance on the one and two.)*

This is very talky compared to my other videos. I use a simple demonstration dance to illustrate how we can dance on the first or the second beat.

Further Ideas: The only reason I have included this lesson is because there are so many people that are passionate that their way is the correct way. I want to prepare my students for this hot topic!

### 2. Some People Cannot Hear nor see the Difference

*(So it's normal if you do not find this useful.)*

If you are left a bit puzzled I suggest moving on and forgetting about this. Simply dance the way you were before!

Further Ideas: I find the underlying reason often varies but the solution is almost always to leave it. If the student cannot sense the difference very clearly I find they are rarely motivated to learn it. If they did want to try to learn it anyway I would encourage them to come back to it a few months later. If they were private students I might try a personalised exercise for two minutes every lesson and with this tailored approach they might get it quickly.

## Section B: Warm Up

Further Ideas: If you are a teacher developing a lesson plan for this, you might start out by dancing on the one for a warm up dance. With improver dancers I would likely leave them to have a practice dance on their own and not actually lead this.

## Section C: New Skills

Further Ideas: As a teacher I might now lead my class dancing individually on the two. I would start with slow music but also try medium-speed music: I find that depending on the student they might pick this up faster with either slow or medium-speed music. The next exercise might be to let them work in couples on their own with music on and I would come round helping.

Further Ideas: Changing between dancing on the one and two during the same dance is not something I have seen people do socially on purpose. I only switch between the two as a practice drill with my students.

## Section D: Dance Naturally

Further Ideas: As a teacher I would usually put some music on and allow my students to practice whatever they wanted. Some might choose not to dance on the two if they don't like it and practice something else instead: I might try to give them a bit of individualised learning input so they also feel they got something useful from them from this lesson (or part of the lesson).

# Copyright and Video Download Link

Copyright 2021 Dr Duncan James

Any questions or comments or just want to chat? Email me (the author) at drduncanjames@gmail.com and I'll do my best to reply.

If you "follow" Duncan James on Amazon you can get updates about new books that I write.

Video Download Link (a zip file of approximately 3GB)
https://u.pcloud.link/publink/show?code=XZKBVmXZrDInssma2ImJC2dGxdmLx4wFz44y

This download is provided by me and is limited by my internet host to a certain number every month and may not work if that limit has been reached. I am happy for you to then share this zip file onwards if you wish as this reduces the pressure on my internet host.

Printed in Great Britain
by Amazon